John Lynch, PhD
Christopher Kilmartin, PhD

The Pain Behind the Mask
Overcoming
Masculine Depression

"**L**ynch and Kilmartin's articulate and profound understanding of men's experience provides insight into men's behavior and offers solutions for helping men who are unhappy find a way out of the male gender dilemma. This book offers a deep and thoughtful analysis of men's behavior and emotions. It should be read by anyone who works with men or who is interested in understanding and curbing men's destructive behavior."

Alan D. Berkowitz, PhD
Independent Consultant;
Student Affairs Staff
Development Consultant,
Wheaton College

"**M**asculine depression remains hidden behind the facades of both male armor and therapeutic inattention. We assume depression is a 'woman's' complaint, and miss the ways in which traditional masculinity often conceals men's depression. Lynch and Kilmartin pierce both the masculine facade and the therapeutic inattention and reveal the depths of despair that men often experience, and the dangerous consequences of keeping it locked inside—for themselves, their loved ones, and society at large. Lynch and Kilmartin possess that rare combination of individual empathy and political vision, which makes *The Pain Behind the Mask* a work of both compassion for men's experiences and uncompromising commitment to gender equality."

Michael Kimmel
Professor, State University
of New York at Stony Brook;
Editor, *Men and Masculinities*

"*The Pain Behind the Mask* is a significant breakthrough in explaining men's depression and it's effects on men's lives and their relationships with others. It is a useful, practical book that will help men and their therapists understand the origins, consequences, and remediations of men's depression. Concisely written and full of intelligible concepts, it will help men assess and change their lives toward greater emotional freedom, intimacy, and self-confidence. The book exposes men's real problems living in a patriarchal society and explains how to turn their pain into positive action and healing."

James M. O'Neil, PhD
Co-Author, *What Causes Men's Violence Against Women*

"Lynch and Kilmartin provide us with a new and exciting means of conceptualizing much of men's unhealthy and damaging behavior. They provide us with effective means for addressing these issues in a manner that can be utilized by mental health professionals, academicians, and the general public."

Robert A. Rando, PhD
Director, University Counseling Center; Assistant Professor, Department of Counseling; Youngstown State University, Youngstown, OH

"*The Pain Behind the Mask* is an eminently useful and readable description and analysis of the many disguised forms of men's emotional pain. The myth of the stoic male, impervious to depression, has been hollowed out by the emerging new discipline of men's studies. Lynch and Kilmartin's book helps fill in the hollowed space with a clearly written and accessible description of the emotional distress experienced by so many men, the origins of such distress, and concrete suggestions for its amelioration. Free of jargon, yet faithful to the complexity of the forces that shape men's emotional lives, *The Pain Behind the Mask* will be a compelling book for spouses and family members of depressed men, as well as for the men themselves. Beyond that, however, this book will also be useful to clinicians. Avoiding linguistic shortcuts, Lynch and Kilmartin have written an engaging and sophisticated exploration of how and why men manifest their emotional distress in the ways they typically do. Clinicians will find in it both a reminder and a guide to searching for the underlying causes of the many disguised behaviors that so often mask men's depression."

David Lisak, PhD
Associate Professor, Clinical Psychologist, Department of Psychology, University of Massachusetts, Boston

More pre-publication
REVIEWS, COMMENTARIES, EVALUATIONS . . .

"**I**n *The Pain Behind the Mask,* Lynch and Kilmartin elucidate the various ways in which men experience and respond to the psychological distress in their lives. Complex intrapersonal and interpersonal dynamics are explained in a readable, concise, and straightforward fashion. This is a book that men and their therapists will find valuable. I recommend it as a bibliotherapy resource."

Glenn G. Good, PhD
Associate Professor,
Educational and Counseling
Psychology, University
of Missouri-Columbia;
President, Society
for the Psychological Study
of Men and Masculinity,
Division 51 of the American
Psychological Association

"**L**ynch and Kilmartin focus on our most destructive social and mental health problem—masculine depression that goes unrecognized and leads to the violence, abuse, and self-neglect that wreck so many lives. Their book could not be clearer or more compassionate. It is right on target and it is sorely needed."

Frank S. Pittman III, MD
Author, *Man Enough: Fathers, Sons and the Search for Masculinity* and *Grow Up! How Taking Responsibility Can Make You a Happy Adult*

"**L**ynch and Kilmartin address a central problem in the contemporary crisis of gender—namely the male tendency to experience depression as a disconnection from self and others. *The Pain Behind the Mask* delineates the damaging effects of unrecognized masculine depression on both women and men, and points the way for how men can heal in the context of relationships. This book is a must read!"

Ronald F. Levant, EdD
Co-Author, *Masculinity Reconstructed;*
Dean, Department of Psychology,
Nova Southeastern University

"**F**inally, a model for understanding what many clinicians have long suspected—that men's destructive behavior and high suicide rates are evidence of underlying depression. With precision and compassion, Lynch and Kilmartin lift off the mask of men's depression. Examining it in the context of men's relationships, they skillfully guide men and their partners, family, friends, and therapists through this uncharted territory, providing practical tools we all need to reduce men's depression and undo its damaging effects."

Will Courtenay, LCSW, PhD
Founder and Director,
Men's Health Consulting,
Berkeley, CA

The Haworth Press, Inc.

The Pain Behind the Mask
Overcoming Masculine Depression

THE HAWORTH PRESS
Advances in Psychology and Mental Health
Frank De Piano, PhD
Senior Editor

Beyond the Therapeutic Relationship: Behavioral, Biological, and Cognitive Foundations of Psychotherapy by Frederic J. Leger

How the Brain Talks to Itself: A Clinical Primer of Psychotherapeutic Neuroscience by Jay E. Harris

Cross-Cultural Counseling: The Arab-Palestinian Case by Marwan Dwairy

The Vulnerable Therapist: Practicing Psychotherapy in an Age of Anxiety by Helen W. Coale

Professionally Speaking: Public Speaking for Health Professionals by Arnold Melnick

Introduction to Group Therapy: A Practical Guide by Scott Simon Fehr

The Pain Behind the Mask: Overcoming Masculine Depression by John Lynch and Christopher Kilmartin

The Pain Behind the Mask
Overcoming Masculine Depression

John Lynch, PhD
Christopher Kilmartin, PhD

The Haworth Press
New York • London • Oxford

The Haworth Press, Inc., 10 Alice Street, Binghamton, NY 13904-1580

Cover design by Marylouise E. Doyle.

Library of Congress Cataloging-in-Publication Data

Lynch, John, 1950-
    The pain behind the mask : overcoming masculine depression / John Lynch, Christopher T. Kilmartin.
        p.   cm.
    Includes bibliographical references and index.
    ISBN 0-7890-0557-3 (alk. paper).
    1. Depression, Mental. 2. Men—Mental health. 3. Men—Psychology. I. Kilmartin, Christopher T. II. Title.
RC537.L94 1999
616.85′27′0081—DC21   98-45944
                                                                                                              CIP

For Mary and Allyson,
who help to open our minds
and our hearts.

ABOUT THE AUTHORS

John Lynch, PhD, is a licensed clinical psychologist in private practice in Richmond, Virginia. With more than twenty years of experience in his field, Dr. Lynch has worked with community service boards to develop treatment programs for victims and perpetrators of domestic violence. He has conducted workshops on providing effective psychotherapy to men individually, in groups, and in relationships. Dr. Lynch has expertise in mind/body therapies, especially in preparation for surgery. He has developed and supervised inpatient treatment programs for clients with dissociative identity disorder. Dr. Lynch has also developed an inpatient psychiatric program for men at the Charter Westbrook Hospital in Virginia. Presently, Dr. Lynch is a member of the American Psychological Association's Society for the Psychological Study of Men and Masculinity.

Christopher Kilmartin, PhD, is Associate Professor of Psychology at Mary Washington College in Fredericksburg, Virginia, and is an expert in the areas of men's issues and violence prevention. Dr. Kilmartin is a licensed clinical psychologist who has a great deal of experience consulting with businesses, college students, human service workers, and counselors. Over the last five years, he has been involved in national leadership of the White Ribbon Campaign, a grassroots effort to decrease men's violence against women. Dr. Kilmartin also consults with campuses and communities who want to start their own White Ribbon Campaign. In addition, he is author of *The Masculine Self* (Macmillan, 1994), a textbook on the psychology of men. Dr. Kilmartin is the author and performer of a solo theatrical performance on masculinity, *Crimes Against Nature.* Currently, Dr. Kilmartin is a member of the American Psychological Association's Society for the Psychological Study of Men and Masculinity and a member of the National Organization for Men Against Sexism.

CONTENTS

Preface

The authors of this book shared all tasks equally. *The Pain Behind the Mask* is a true collaboration between professionals (and friends) with complementary strengths. John Lynch is a full-time psychotherapist and a part-time scholar; Christopher Kilmartin is a full-time scholar and a part-time psychotherapist. Both of us have been involved in a serious examination of men's roles in society for well over a decade.

The goal of this book is to introduce an expanded view of depression that accounts for men's disturbing behaviors in relationships. We have tried to present these ideas in down-to-earth language so that they will be accessible to the men's studies scholar as well as to the person who has relatively little experience in understanding the gendered aspects of men's experience.

This is both a professional and a self-help book. Psychotherapists will find useful ways to conceptualize and intervene with clients who display the symptoms of masculine depression. Laypersons will be able to understand and solve the problems that may affect them and/or the men in their lives. The question-and-answer format is intended to guide the reader as we explore various subtopics within each general area.

We have included many case examples throughout to illustrate various characteristics and dynamics of masculine depression. These cases are descriptions of actual men whom we have known as clients, friends, and acquaintances. We have presented the struggles and psychological processes of these men as accurately as possible. However, we have changed the details of their lives (their names, occupations, ethnicities, etc.) to disguise their identities. Therefore, any resemblance of these cases to actual people is coincidental. As we describe ourselves as therapists, we use the first person singular because, while it is important to describe these men's struggles, it is unimportant to identify which of us undertook treatment with each man. In the instances in which we discuss our personal lives, we identify ourselves with our initials in parentheses, as is the convention for a co-authored volume.

This book is the product of seven years of writing, researching, talking, and developing. We endured many setbacks and produced many revisions in the process. The difficulties that we encountered tested our resolve and forced us to continually refine our ideas. In acknowledging the help that we have received, we wish first to acknowledge each other. This book has been a collaborative effort between two men with strong opinions, and it was quite a challenge to develop a manuscript that brings together the strengths and unique views that each of us has to offer. We were able to work together and find ways to communicate both our commonly held views and our differences. As men, we were committed to resolving our disputes fairly. Our friendship has grown and deepened as a result.

We wish to offer our most sincere acknowledgments to our partners. Mary provided John with vital discussions and counterpoints, editing help, and invaluable time free from family chores to write. Allyson also supported Chris in his time investment and other struggles involved in the preparation of the manuscript. For years, both of these wonderful women have enriched our understanding of gender through numerous personal and scholarly conversations. Mary's expertise as a developmental psychologist and Allyson's proficiency as a social historian have contributed immeasurably to our own sophistication as counseling psychologists.

We were blessed with readers who took our work seriously and devoted themselves to a thorough and thoughtful reading of our manuscript. They helped us to refine our statements and pointed out when our zeal took us too far from the topic. We wish to thank Jan Altman, Paul Isely, Richard Edelman, Jennifer Edelman, Linda LaFave, and Edith Ott for their interest in this project and all of their thoughtful reactions to the manuscript. Thanks also to Paul Isely for preparing our illustrations.

John Lynch
Christopher Kilmartin

Introduction

The central premise of this book is that a great deal of depression in men is misunderstood and misdiagnosed. For many men, sadness and despair find a distorted expression in immature, aloof, selfish, or cruel behaviors that disguise their emotional pain to others and even to themselves. Because it is so difficult to see the pain behind the mask, people tend to deal solely with the outward appearance of the problem behavior and fail to address its underlying causes. As a result, masculine depression often goes unrecognized and untreated.

This book is the product of several years of thinking about men and depression in the contexts of scholarly works we have read, men we have known, clients we have seen professionally, and our own personal experiences. We have organized what we have learned into a model of masculine depression that will address the needs of three groups:

1. Men who are experiencing the symptoms that we describe
2. People who find that they have to deal with someone who has these symptoms within the context of a close relationship
3. Professionals who seek guidance in treating masculine depression

We will present a model that provides new ways of understanding men's behavior. No model says it all, and so it is important that readers understand the context and limitations of our model before reading on.

We will be describing a style of depression that is manifested by two basic and related characteristics: *dissociation from feelings* and *destructive behavior in relationships. Dissociation* refers to a process by which a person loses awareness of natural human reactions and inner experiences. In the case of many depressed men, dissociation involves the disconnection of their feelings from conscious experience.

This process leads to the second characteristic, *destructive behavior in relationships.* Life is hard, and it is inevitable that a person will have stressful and hurtful experiences from time to time. Because depressed males are so likely to dissociate from their feelings, they tend to carry the emotional pain from these experiences into their relationships with their wives, children, and friends. The result is a variety of destructive behaviors: interpersonal distancing, emotional bullying, neglect, and violence. The relationships in a man's life are also disturbed indirectly by several other common manifestations of masculine depression, including substance abuse, physical health difficulties, workaholism, and unnecessary risk taking.

A model is an organized way of thinking about a complex problem. Our goal in presenting this model of masculine depression is to clearly identify the nature of the problem and to suggest solutions that follow from our conceptualization of the issue. We do not seek to make men victims; we seek to describe men's responsibility and propose realistic strategies for change.

The limitations of our model are as follows. First, it is not a description of all men, all of the time. Many men have fulfilling relationships with their partners and children, rich emotional lives, and deep friendships. Although some aspects of traditional masculinity encourage men to become dissociated from their feelings and destructive in their relationships, these outcomes are not inevitable.

Second, we will be describing a style of depression that is common in men, but not universal. Some men show the classic symptoms we have come to associate with depression, and there are also women who have the "masculine" symptom pattern that is the focus of this book.

Third, although we include research findings where applicable, this model is not completely derived from empirical sources—controlled experiments, statistical analyses, and a systematic investigation of scientific claims. It is constructed from our work with clients in our professional roles as clinical psychologists, our knowledge of the research, our experiences of living in the world as men, and our understanding of the influence of gender demands in men's lives. The value of any model is in its usefulness. If we can help people think about men's problems in a way that leads to workable solutions, then we will have done our job well.

The focus of this model is limited. For reasons that will become apparent, we have chosen to place our emphasis on a man's healing within the context of his relationships as an adult—typically, those with his partner, his children, and other men, as well as his relationship with himself. We know that these are not the only important areas for men's work. There are several excellent books that address other contexts of men's healing. For example, Terrence Real's *I Don't Want to Talk About It*[1] emphasizes solutions to masculine depression in the worlds of individual therapy and the inward journey of self-exploration. In *Finding Our Fathers,* Sam Osherson[2] looks at men's efforts to deal directly with the powerful emotional relationships that most men have with their fathers.

Our work is mainly focused on heterosexual men. Many gay and bisexual men have problems similar to the ones we describe and can benefit from our presentation of issues in masculine development. However, their status as sexual minorities creates some other issues as well. A number of outstanding writers (e.g., Greg Herek,[3] Warren Blumenfeld,[4] and Martin Duberman[5]) are engaged in the ongoing process of addressing these issues.

We will be describing ways in which men's emotional pain leads to destructive behaviors in relationships. Do not be misled into thinking that we are *excusing* these behaviors. Many men behave in ways that cause women, children, and other men to suffer horribly. Nothing can condone or justify this behavior, and no cause for the behavior absolves men of the responsibility for its consequences. We seek to understand the roots of the problem so that men can be guided in their efforts toward responsible change. Rather than pathologizing men, we seek to help them to find full and healthy expressions of their humanity.

Masculine depression is a condition that is brought on by conflicting needs and manifested in disturbed behavior in relationships. In Part I (Chapters 1 through 4), we describe the symptoms of masculine depression, its origins, and its consequences. Social forces often demand that males withhold the expression of feelings that cannot be withheld, be autonomous and masterful without any real model to guide them, display no doubt or hesitation even when they are doubtful and unsure, and appear completely independent from women while at the same time depending on women to validate their masculinity. The negative effects of these conflicting needs are manifested in the defensive, guarded, and victimizing relationships that men undertake in order to avoid exposing their weaknesses. Many disturbed men behave in disturbing ways.

Once we gain insight into the origins of masculine depression, we can describe the changes that will provide effective relief. In our model, these origins are in relationships. This understanding helps us to build a bridge between problem and solution. Part II (Chapters 5 through 10) provides a sequence of remedies that follow from the model presented in Part I. Relationships in daily life offer men the opportunity to express their full humanity. Men can learn to recover their emotional lives, deal with their unstated fear of other men, negotiate intimacy with their partners, and participate fully in their children's lives. Those who do so overcome the two defining characteristics of masculine depression: dissociation from feelings and destructive behavior in relationships.

This book is a product of several years of conversation between the two of us and with many others, especially our partners. In the process of writing and talking, both of us have felt our personal and professional lives blending together. Like all men, we grew up and live in a world that encourages us to be traditionally masculine at every turn. We are aware that part of the great social force of gender is the pressure to keep our feelings to ourselves and to be less involved in home and family than our partners. It seems to us that these gender demands have their own momentum. When we do not understand these pressures, we are often swept along by gender arrangements, unaware that we have choices about how we behave.

This book comes from both the head and the heart. The ideas that we discuss with each other are grounded in our everyday experiences. Our conversations have highlighted the pervasiveness of masculine gender demands in the world of our daily experiences and strengthened our commitment to live our lives in ways that reflect our values, regardless of whether or not these behaviors fit the prescribed social roles of men.

As we continue to understand the pressure to be traditionally masculine, we also reaffirm our choice to be otherwise. As a result of the conversations that have become this book, we feel more connected, centered, and satisfied with our efforts to express our humanity. We have seen our relationships become increasingly rich. It is our fond hope that reading this book will have as positive an effect for you as writing it has for us.

PART I:
ORIGINS AND CONSEQUENCES

Chapter 1

He Sure Doesn't Look Depressed

Appearances can be deceiving. When a magician shows someone the technique behind a magic trick, the illusion becomes easier to understand. The same is true for the world of human behavior. Sometimes, mental health problems are also illusory, and when we can grasp the origins of these problems, we are in a better position to solve them. For instance, psychologists have learned that some elderly people show symptoms of dementia ("senility" or Alzheimer's disease) when, in fact, they are depressed. Treat the person for depression, and the dementia is cured. Sometimes people become psychotic (lose touch with reality) because of negative reactions to prescription drugs. If the drug is discontinued, the psychotic behavior disappears.

Appearances can be extremely deceiving when behaviors are profound distortions of underlying problems. Consider the following three cases:

> Andy is a thirty-one-year-old corporate manager who batters his wife physically and emotionally. Their relationship follows a predictable pattern—they argue over little things, and the tension between them builds for several days until Andy "blows up." On some occasions, he has hurt his wife so badly that she has had to be hospitalized. She has left him several times, but he has always been able to "charm" her back. In the days that follow the beating incidents, Andy is extremely remorseful. He apologizes profusely, brings home flowers, and takes his wife out to dinner at fine restaurants. But this honeymoon period never lasts for more than a few days. Soon the conflict begins to escalate, and it always culminates in another beating episode. Andy may want to love his wife consistently in "normal" ways, but he finds it impossible to do so.

* * *

Danny is a thirty-six-year-old auto mechanic who works at a car dealership five days a week and also operates his own auto repair business out of his garage. There is rarely a waking moment when Danny is not fixing a car; he works every evening and all day on the weekends. His goal is to retire at age forty-five, and he is making quite a bit of money in this quest. But all is not well. He suffers from chronic lower back pain, and he has put off seeking treatment for this condition for years. His wife and children frequently complain about his lack of involvement with the family. Danny becomes enraged at the suggestion that he is not a good husband or father. He is an excellent financial provider. In his mind, this is the essence of the man's role in the family. Danny firmly believes that he is doing the right thing, and he cannot understand how his wife and children can have any different perspective.

* * *

Alan is a forty-two-year-old lawyer who portrays himself as the successful playboy. Although he has never had a long-term relationship, he rarely has any trouble finding women to date because of his physical attractiveness and his social status. He brags of his sexual conquests and never lets on to his male friends that he has a vague sense that something is missing in his life. His parents continually suggest that he "find a nice girl and settle down," but Alan tells them that "I'm a dater, not a relater." His reputation for lying to women has tarnished his social and professional image. Any discomfort he feels simply propels him to find another dating partner.

What do these three men have in common? First and foremost, they are all harmful to other people. Andy hurts his wife physically and emotionally. She lives in terror of the next attack. Danny is distant from his family, who need his attention and love. Alan has made a career out of exploiting and hurting women emotionally. Second, there is a good deal of destructive anger in the lives of all three men. It is obvious for the physically violent Andy. Danny becomes extraordinarily angry when his wife and children criticize his lack of involvement with them. Alan's rage is more passive and subtle. He entices women into the hope of a relationship, and then he inflicts emotional pain on them by mistreating and abandoning them. A third common thread among these men is that they all experience a level of personal discomfort. Andy is very uncomfortable with the rising tension between him and his wife, and he hates himself after he has been violent. Danny is in actual physical discomfort in addition to the emotional pain he experiences when he feels unappreciated by his family. Alan is bothered by his negative reputation and a vague sense of emptiness in his life. Each man handles his emotional discomfort in ways that we have come to view as "masculine"—aggressive, distant, and/or sexually permissive. Each man engages in these destructive behaviors in a repetitive way; each is locked into a rigid pattern that creates problems and solves none.

This leads us to one very important commonality among the three people described above: they are all male. This fact should not be surprising, given the typically masculine characteristics of their behaviors. However, when we search for similarities among these three cases, the word "depression" does not readily spring to mind. After all, these men do not cry all day, have trouble eating, miss work, or brood about their problems. If you asked them, they won't tell you that they feel hopeless, helpless, or worthless. In fact, most of the people around them are not aware that these men are experiencing any personal discomfort whatsoever. Much of the time, the men themselves are not aware of it either. He sure doesn't *look* depressed to others, or even to himself. Maybe we do not see them as depressed because our ideas about depression are limited and misleading when it comes to these men's symptoms. Although it is hard to see the pain behind the mask, each of these men is depressed.

WHAT IS DEPRESSION?

Depression is often referred to as the "common cold" of mental illness, affecting ten million people at any given time in the United States alone.[1] The classic symptoms are well known: feelings of sadness, helplessness, and hopelessness, changes in eating and sleeping patterns, low self-esteem, lack of energy, crying, and isolating oneself from others.[2] Many psychologists and psychiatrists believe that depression is a collection of symptoms that results from some kind of unresolved conflict.

In addition to the severe human suffering that accompanies this disorder, the effects of depression cost businesses untold billions in lost productivity and absenteeism. As striking as these figures are, they may be a gross underestimate of the problem. Many mental health experts agree that a large population of depressed men and women, even those with access to the health care system, go undiagnosed and untreated. We believe that a disproportionate number of these people are men. We also suggest that, in addition to problems with worker morale, depression is strongly linked to the most serious social problem in the United States today: violence—with its staggering physical, emotional, and financial costs.

How Does Depression Relate to Being Masculine or Feminine?

Current statistics indicate that women are diagnosed with depression twice as often as men.[3] A careful examination of the *Diagnostic and Statistical Manual of Mental Disorders* (DSM-IV)[4] reveals why this is so. This book, published by the American Psychiatric Association, has long provided standard symptom lists for various psychological problems. Its criteria for Major Depression are as follows:

- depressed mood
- diminished pleasure in activities
- significant weight loss (when not dieting) or weight gain
- insomnia (trouble sleeping) or hypersomnia (sleeping too much)
- psychomotor agitation (nervousness and restlessness) or retardation (sluggishness)
- fatigue or loss of energy
- feelings of worthlessness or guilt
- diminished ability to concentrate, or indecisiveness
- recurrent thoughts of death (Reprinted with permission from the *Diagnostic and Statistical Manual of Mental Disorders,* Fourth Edition. Copyright 1994 American Psychiatric Association.)

If we look closely at these criteria, we see that they describe a typical depressed *woman.* It may be that women are diagnosed as depressed more often than men because the diagnostic criteria for depression are biased toward the kind of depression that women tend to experience and express in our culture: feelings of sadness and guilt, worrying, crying, self-blaming, and moping. This pattern is sometimes referred to as "acting in" because the focus is on internal feelings rather than external behaviors. Women often "act in" because of a cultural gender role that emphasizes both the expression of feeling and a focus on internal judgments of their own inadequacies. In the feminine mode of depression, conflicts are expressed in a fairly direct way. A diagram of femine depression looks like this:

CONFLICT --->   NEGATIVE EMOTION --->   CLASSIC DEPRESSION

(psychological loss)   (sadness)   (feeling sad, lack of energy and interests)

WHAT IS MASCULINE DEPRESSION?

Almost everybody knows that it is considered unmanly to act in the way we have just described: crying, moping, and expressing doubts about oneself. So, when men experience emotional pain, they tend to react with anger, self-destructiveness, and/or by distracting themselves with behaviors such as drinking (or other drug use), gambling, womanizing, and workaholism. Because men are raised to be independent, active, task oriented, and successful, they tend to express painful feelings by blaming others, denying their feelings, and finding solutions for their problems in places outside of themselves. Whereas women tend to "act in" in reaction to negative feelings, men tend to "act out." Most depressed men are not even aware of their depression, because they are very disconnected from their feelings and because their behaviors do not have the "typical" depressed appearance.

Why Does Emotional Disconnection Occur More Frequently in Men Than in Women?

Men and women tend to display different depressive styles because of *gender socialization,* a process that encourages individuals to operate in the world according to explicit or implicit rules based on being female or male. Females are usually raised to be feeling oriented, introspective, noncompetitive, and focused on helping others. Males are frequently raised to be self-focused, task oriented, active, and independent. When something goes wrong in women's lives, their development leads them to first look for their own failures, to focus on relationship losses, and to express their painful feelings. In contrast, men are encouraged to seek explanations and solutions for depression in the external world and to emphasize the control, not the expression, of emotion. With these very disparate styles in mind, it is easy to see how the same inner experience of conflict, hopelessness, and helplessness can lead to very different, seemingly unconnected behaviors in a man and a woman.

Men face a wide range of emotions, but they are also conditioned to neither experience these feelings nor reveal them to others. Men seek and need intimate relationships in order to survive psychologically, but the skills and behaviors required for an intimate relationship are opposite from the set of defensive behaviors known as *traditional masculinity*—the characteristic response to the demands to be hyperindependent, unfeeling, unfeminine, and powerful at all times. Over years of psychological development, men have learned to detach themselves from the awareness of vulnerable feelings. Thus, men frequently do not develop the vocabulary or awareness necessary for the verbal expression of feelings. As a result, an emotional void exists in the lives of many men.

In place of emotional awareness, masculinity stresses competition, toughness, hyperindependence ("I can handle it by myself"), and accomplishment. If asked, "How do you feel?" men learn to reply, "About what?" and then tell you what they *think*. If asked to talk about their wives or girlfriends, men learn to deny the importance of such intimate relationships because they are being asked about the very feelings that they have been conditioned to avoid. After all, so-called "real men" are not supposed to be vulnerable, sentimental, or attached.

Although masculinity limits the direct expression of feeling, these emotions are still expressed in one way or another. Feelings can be expressed in three basic ways. One is a direct, conscious expression in relation to the source of the feeling. For instance, a man could tell his wife that he feels angry or disappointed when she always seems to be on the phone with her sister during dinner. The other two expressions of feelings are indirect, presenting themselves either as changes in behavior or as physical symptoms. For instance, this same man might yell at his children or suddenly develop stomach cramps in response to his wife's behavior. Too often, we focus solely on men's behavior and ignore the underlying emotional experience that is expressed in that behavior.

We see the indirect effect of negative emotional experience in some of the typical physical illnesses suffered more frequently by men than women: low back pain, heart disease, ulcers, even cancer. Although all of these problems have physiological bases, many studies have documented psychological contributions to these illnesses as well. At times, the man's body knows something that he does not know consciously.

HOW IS MASCULINE DEPRESSION DIFFERENT FROM FEMININE DEPRESSION?

Feminine depression is expressed in the ways that we have come to associate with a typical depression. The following outline identifies the major features of feminine depression:

DIRECT EXPRESSION OF FEELINGS
(experiencing and talking about emotional pain)

↗

FEMININE DEPRESSION

↘

"ACTING IN" BEHAVIORS
(crying, moping, loss of pleasure, insomnia)

These characteristics stand in stark contrast to the features of masculine depression. An outline of the major features of masculine depression reveals the following:

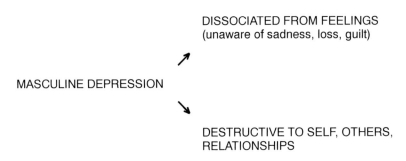

MASCULINE DEPRESSION

DISSOCIATED FROM FEELINGS
(unaware of sadness, loss, guilt)

DESTRUCTIVE TO SELF, OTHERS, RELATIONSHIPS

We will refer to these two major characteristics of masculine depression throughout this book. *Dissociation* from feelings refers to a process in which one loses conscious awareness of one's emotional states. Men are often encouraged to do so through the masculine socialization process and problematic family dynamics that we will be describing throughout Part I of this book. As you will see, dissociated feelings find expression in ways that are *destructive to self, others, and relationships*. Problematic behaviors in this area include being aloof with one's partner, distant from one's children, unable to form meaningful friendships, taking unnecessary risks with one's health, and being overly aggressive in a variety of ways.

The masculine and feminine styles that we have described are both expressions of depression, but they have little else in common. They do not look like, feel like, or present themselves as the same condition. Yet both styles are symptoms of similar underlying problems. It is easy to see the first style as depression. Indeed, it is what the psychiatric community has come to define as depression. The second style, seen in a social context, is most frequently described in terms that do not include depression. Rather than describing these behaviors as "troubled" or depressed, too often we have labeled them only by their social effects: antisocial, distant, and obnoxious.

What Are the Symptoms of Masculine Depression?

If the surface appearance is so different from the underlying dynamics of depression, how can a man tell if he is struggling with depression? How can his wife or friends tell? Consider the following questions.

- Do you lose your temper easily?
- Do you get into arguments at home after a bad day at work?
- Do you behave aggressively after a significant loss (of a job, relationship, etc.)?
- Do you engage in activities that have a high potential for physical injury?
- Do you drink too much or use other drugs?
- Do you experience a vague sense that something is wrong, but are unable to express it?
- Do you neglect your physical health?
- Do you feel emotionally numb?
- Does your wife or partner identify your feelings better than you do?
- Do you push, hit, or emotionally abuse your wife or partner, come close to it, or feel strong impulses to do so?
- Do you obsessively distract yourself through work or sports?
- Are you described as being "cold" or "overly logical"?
- Do you have few or no close friends?
- Does your partner complain that you run away when she gets too close?
- Does the breakup of an intimate relationship make you miss work, drink heavily, or become desperate to find a new relationship?
- Do your children fear you when you are in a bad mood?
- Does your family hide important information from you to "keep the peace?"

Are <u>All</u> Men Depressed?

If you look at the previous list, it might seem as if most men you know are depressed, and we can't emphasize enough that this is not the case. Like everyone, men have their ups and downs. Most men are able to deal effectively with their lives. Difficulties occur when men experience stress, loss, or the complexities of intimate relationships. This list contains characteristics of so many men because it describes the typical way in which men tend to cope emotionally. We are not describing all men, all of the time. Masculine depression can be an outcome of the rigors of male development for many men, but it is not the only outcome. Many men lead healthy, fulfilling lives. We seek to describe what may be happening when masculine behavior is no longer adaptive, effective, or healthy. We would say that a man is depressed when the behaviors we have described above become a characteristic, self-defeating, and interpersonally disturbing way of handling problems.

Do Only Males Have This Kind of Depression?

This book is not intended to describe a global male experience or to assign masculine depression to all men. The two defining characteristics of masculine depression—dissociating from feelings and destructive behavior—identify our intended audience.

People who show the depressive style described here are mostly males, and the reasons for this gender difference will become obvious as you read further. However, some males who get depressed show symptoms similar to those that we have described as "feminine." And, some women have masculine styles of behavior and personality, which may include the depressive style that is seen more commonly in men. It is important to acknowledge that individuals vary to a great extent; our purpose is to describe a common, but not necessarily universal, problem for men.

If These Depressive Styles Are So Different, What Makes Them Both "Depression"?

Depression is centered around feelings of hopelessness, helplessness, worthlessness, and psychological loss. Consciously or unconsciously, depressed people experience themselves as being fundamentally deficient in some important way. They experience the world as a hostile, unsafe, or unsympathetic place, and they think that the future holds no possibility of being better than the past. People experiencing this kind of pain are depressed. However, what people *do* about their pain differs from person to person, and men tend to react differently than women.

Pain provides information. It tells us something about the world and our relationship to it. Whether it is emotional or physical, pain is nature's way of telling us that something is wrong, and we use that information to adjust accordingly. We see a clear example of the informative value of pain in children who, because of a congenital defect, are unable to sense any physical pain. This might sound like a wonderful attribute to have when you have a bad headache, but in fact it creates profound problems. Because these children receive no feedback from their bodies about what hurts and what does not, they are constantly breaking bones and incurring severe cuts and bruises. They must wear helmets and body pads to protect themselves from severe injury. From moment to moment, we all shift our body positions in response to pain that is so slight that we do not even notice it. People who cannot experience pain can stand in one position for so long that they damage their joints. Disconnected from the experience of physical pain, there is nothing they can do internally to prevent this unintended self-destruction. Protection must come from the outside.[5]

We can see the parallel with emotional pain. Emotional disconnection may make us a little more comfortable in the moment, but we pay a price for this momentary comfort when we lose the informational quality of the pain. In other words, when we do not know what is wrong, we cannot do much to fix it or prevent it from happening in the future.

Many men are quite good at disconnecting themselves from pain because they have practiced doing so for a lifetime, as illustrated by the following scenario. A boy falls and cuts his knee. He is in pain, and he has a natural, human reaction to that pain—he cries. An adult or peer responds with the stereotypical directive, "big boys don't cry." Now he is faced with a choice: he can either follow the natural tendency to express his physical and emotional pain, or he can obey the cultural directive to deny the pain and "get over it."

Sometimes the pain is more purely emotional, as when boys are rejected by friends or ignored by their fathers. These incidents occur again and again in the lives of boys. They are all part of the masculine training for becoming a so-called "real man" (a terminology we dislike intensely; *all* men are real men). The cumulative effect of this training is to distance the male from a basic part of himself. He puts on a mask of bravado, and he becomes so adept at wearing it that he finds it difficult to remove it or to gain emotional access to what is underneath. Through years of socialization, emotions become vague, diffuse, or even nonexistent. He learns to behave like a man, yet the pain behind the mask continues to exist within him, and this pain has a psychological energy of its own.

The bottom line is this: pain affects people. Because it has an effect, pain has to be expressed in some way. In the case of classic (feminine) depression, that expression is fairly direct and easy to understand. On the other hand, masculine depression is often disguised in physical illnesses or destructive behaviors. Even the mental health community fails to recognize that masculine depression—undiagnosed and untreated—exists in huge quantity. Masculine and feminine depression share similar origins in important experiences of psychological loss and emotional trauma. They share similar dynamics in the conscious or unconscious experiences of hopelessness, helplessness, and feelings of low self-esteem.

How Does Masculine Depression Create Problems in Relationships?

Consider the following example:

> Ed's wife had tried to "get through to him" for years. Ed was abusive and neglectful to her. He yelled at his son for the slightest infractions, and he devoted himself to his work, largely to the exclusion of family or leisure. Ed was unaware that these behaviors were strongly influenced by the childhood experience of abuse that he suffered at the hands of his father, whose physical punishing was so frequent and severe that Ed had *dissociated* it from his everyday consciousness. As a child, Ed received and

internalized almost daily messages from his father that he was worthless as a human being. Ed was powerless to do anything to protect himself emotionally, except to escape in his mind during the beatings. Without realizing it, Ed had internalized a sense that he was helpless and worthless, and that the future held no promise for improvement. Ed was depressed, but he hid his pain, even from himself.

Ed had learned that feeling is equal to pain and vulnerability. Because of the severe, unacknowledged pain created by childhood abuse and the cultural dictate for men to avoid feelings, Ed tended to escape from any kind of emotional experience. His behavior resulted in a growing emotional distance between Ed and his wife and son. Ed's wife suffered the brunt of his abuse, and she periodically threatened to leave. Every time she made this threat, he would promise to change, but once the crisis was over, he resorted to the "same old stuff."

After one particularly intense conflict, Ed's wife firmly announced, "It's over, I've had enough." Somehow, this time Ed understood. He saw with horror the effects of his behavior on his family. He saw the ways his father had treated him reflected in his treatment of his own son. He felt the deep sadness, loss, and anger he had hidden from himself all those years. He was now in crisis, alone in the world—his pain open, raw, and unbearable. Finally he had broken through destructive masculinity and was truly willing to address the behaviors. He needed comfort and help from his wife.

However, she was unmoved. She did not take him back, but instead said "I'm sorry you feel so bad; I'm sorry it took so long for you to see it, but I don't have anything left. I really don't know if I'll ever want this marriage back. Right now, I don't." He was panic stricken, and unable to handle his depression about the sudden loss in his life. He pleaded with her, but could not change her decision. In a moment of pure desperation, he said "Fine, then—I'll just blow my brains out; then you'll be happy." (He had no intention of doing so.)

Ed's wife reported this statement to me as evidence of the same old "control and bully tactics" she had experienced from him before. Certainly Ed's threat had the effect his wife described. He was seeking to control his wife, hold her responsible for his pain, ignore her feelings, and bully her back into the relationship. He was having a "masculine panic attack." Flooded with his emotional pain and dependence on his wife, his anxiety became so overwhelming that he feared he could not make it another moment. Instead of hyperventilating, shaking, and having a facial expression of sheer terror, Ed expressed his panic attack in masculine form. He dissociated from the fear that he felt and acted it out in a destructive manner. Later, when asked directly, Ed recognized and talked about the anxiety and panic he felt when he faced that moment alone.

Vulnerable emotions such as anxiety or sadness are experiences that men are not supposed to feel or admit. Yet they are a normal part of life, especially for men such as Ed who have been abused. When powerful feelings are blocked from conscious expression, they tend to "leak out" in the form of abusive relationship behaviors. And, because depressed men tend to see their problems as external to themselves, they are unlikely to change without a compelling reason to do so (such as a partner's threat of abandonment) and a strong motivation to address the internal origins of their difficulties.

How Is Depression Related to the Psychiatric Diagnoses Typically Assigned to Men?

Men are diagnosed as antisocial, substance abusers, and narcissistic more often than women.[6] These diagnoses reflect habitual dissociation from feelings and an acting out of internal conflicts in destructive ways. Substance abuse is frequently described as an attempt at self-medicating. If feelings are numbed and one is filled with chemical euphoria, chronic emptiness and other feared emotions cannot fully surface. Although substance abuse generally leads to more alienation, depression, and anxiety, it is an effective temporary strategy for dealing with feelings of alienation, depression, and anxiety.

Antisocial individuals lack remorse for their actions and are concerned with meeting their own needs. How their behaviors affect others is not in their scope of awareness. They are described as having an impaired or absent conscience. Their behavior is governed not by what is right and wrong, but by what feels good or feels bad for them. Their view of life is narrowed and extends only as far as their own needs. Treatment is difficult as they see no problem and therefore are not motivated to change. Antisocial individuals have often suffered severe childhood abuse and dissociated from it in such an extreme way that they are incapable of forming any kind of truly reciprocal relationship. They engage in behaviors that violate the rights of others; many spend their lives in prison.

We have saved our in-depth discussion of narcissism for Chapter 7 because, for heterosexual men, it frequently surfaces in disturbed relationships with women. For now, it will suffice to say that narcissists suffer from low self-esteem and defend themselves against the accompanying emotional discomfort by bragging, exploiting others, and displaying a grandiose image. Unable to truly relate to others who have their own needs, thoughts, and desires, the narcissist uses relationships for shallow self-aggrandizement. Because the partners of narcissists frequently become angry and weary of being exploited, and because they eventually "see through" the narcissistic defense, these relationships are often volatile and short-lived.

The underlying but unseen origin of all three of these disorders is a pervasive, unconscious sense of hopelessness, helplessness, and worthlessness. Because individuals with these disorders have great difficulty acknowledging these feelings, they cannot gain insight into their problems nor change the behaviors that severely and negatively affect the quality of their lives and the lives of the people with whom they come into contact.

What Evidence Shows That Masculine Depression Really Exists?

If you asked the average man about his mental health, he would probably tell you that he is fine. Yet there are data indicating that, as a group, men suffer from at least as many mental health problems as women.[7] We find the most compelling evidence for the prevalence of undiagnosed masculine depression in three important areas: sex differences in suicide rates, psychiatric hospitalization for divorced men, and sex differences in longevity.

Suicide is the ultimate expression of hopelessness and helplessness. The person who commits this act is telling the world that only death can end the excruciating emotional pain of living. What could be a more obvious sign of depression? *In the United States, males commit suicide four times more often than females.*[8] Male teenagers account for 90 percent of completed suicides in their age group.[9] Among the elderly, the ratio of male to female suicides is an incredible 10 to 1.[10] Except in relatively rare cases of intractable illness or heroic sacrifice, suicide is the clearest indicator of severe depression. An alarming number of males, severely depressed but unable to talk about it for fear of appearing unmasculine, see suicide as their only alternative.

Another sign of extreme depression is the so-called "nervous break-down," in which a person loses his or her ability to cope in the world and has to be admitted to a psychiatric hospital. Sometimes these incidents are triggered by traumatic events in the person's life, such as the death of a loved one or some other profound emotional loss. One of the most severe of these losses involves marital separation or the breakup of a primary, intimate relationship. Surprisingly, *divorced men undergo psychiatric hospitalization at eight times the rate of married men*[11] and have more psychological difficulties than women in adjusting to divorce and separation.[12] Although we tend to think of men as independent, this fact suggests otherwise. Many men depend on their wives to manage their emotional lives for them. When a breakup occurs, they are left alone with their pain and are incompetent to manage these feelings without a great deal of help.

Men also die an average of seven years earlier than women.[13] There are a number of reasons for this, and some are biological (e.g., testosterone's negative effect on cholesterol levels).[14] However, many of the reasons for the gendered lifespan differential are not biological. They are related to behaviors that are linked to masculinity. For instance, men smoke more, drink more, eat less healthful foods, take more physical risks, and engage in violent behaviors more often than women.[15] Men are more likely to refuse or delay seeing a physician when they have health problems and they are more likely to under report their symptoms to doctors.[16] Recent research also indicates that chronic anger increases the risk of stroke (cerebrovascular accident) after age fifty.[17] As anger is the only socially accepted male emotion, it is reasonable to suggest (as we will throughout this book) that much of men's anger is converted from depressed feelings. We may also infer that other self-destructive behaviors contain significant depressive components. Mounting evidence suggests that expressing depression through destructive or neglectful behaviors is hazardous to men's health.

These statistics present quite a paradox. On the one hand, women are diagnosed as depressed much more often than men. On the other hand, men outpace women, far and away, in two of the strongest indicators of depression, and they die younger. How can it be that women are more depressed than men, but men show stronger signs of depression than women? As we have stated, the answer is that the diagnostic criteria for depression are biased toward the kind of depression that women tend to experience and express. But the underlying feelings of all depressed people are the same. For many men, however, the expression of these feelings is so distorted that the depression becomes unrecognizable.

Masculine gender role demands dictate that men *never* deal with any emotions (except for anger and sexual feelings). Men are socialized to ignore their feelings and to *do* something when they have a problem. As a sense of worthlessness, hopelessness, and helplessness finds its way into the man's psyche, he experiences a sometimes vague sense of being vulnerable and endangered. Because he has neither the awareness nor the skills to deal with this sense in a direct way, he learns how to distance himself from his feelings using a variety of strategies. Because many of these feelings are painful, and because he has learned that "real men" *think* and *do* rather than *feel* and *experience*, he shuts down large portions of his emotional life, usually without much conscious awareness that he is doing so. He has divorced emotion from reason, as he learned to do from the culture of masculinity.

But as an old psychoanalytic saying goes, "Emotion never lies; emotion never lies still." Powerful feelings cry for expression, and because most men have not learned to deal with their experiences directly, they do so indirectly through destructive behaviors. The victim can be another person, as is the case with violent behaviors, and/or it can be himself, as with self-destructive behaviors such as excessive drinking or physical illnesses that have psychological origins. The masculine mode of depression looks like this:

CONFLICT --->	DISSOCIATION --->	MASCULINE ---> DEPRESSION	DESTRUCTIVE-NESS
(psychological loss)	(ignore or deny sadness)	(indirect expression)	(violence, neglect, or self-destruc-tiveness)

How Is Disconnection from Feelings Involved in Hurting Others?

As an illustration of the way in which this entire indirect process affects destructive behaviors, we can look at the all-too-frequent case of the person who is abused as a child and later grows up to become a child abuser. Most people are surprised to find that a history of child abuse is common among adults who abuse children. After all, shouldn't a person who knows what it is like to be a victim be especially careful not to victimize others? The following case illustrates the process by which a person develops from a victim into a perpetrator of abuse.

Bart is a self-employed man in his mid-forties. If you saw him, you might think of him as a classic "hippie"—long hair, tattoos, and tattered blue jeans. He has fathered several children with different wives, but only one child, a son, currently lives with him. Bart abused marijuana and alcohol up until his early forties, when he stopped due to the urgings of his live-in girlfriend and an incident in which his substance abuse almost cost him his business. He was also under the scrutiny of the criminal justice system because social services determined that he had physically abused his son.

In a family therapy session that was focused on changing Bart's pattern of "discipline," he said, "I'm raising my son the same way I was raised." He went on to say that, "My father used to take me out to the shed and whip me so badly that I would bleed." When the therapist replied, "I'm sorry that happened to you," he looked surprised for just an instant, then he said, "It was the *best thing that ever happened to me.*"

Photographs of Bart's son's bruised body on file at the Social Services office make it hard to believe that this kind of experience could possibly be positive in any sense at all.

How could Bart be so blind about his own pain, much less that of his son? We are tempted to make the easy explanation that this abusive behavior is a result of pure imitation. As indicated by Bart's statements, he was merely emulating the style of discipline that his father modeled for him. To an extent, this explanation is surely part of what has happened, but it cuts much deeper than that. Because Bart learned how to shut down his own pain after so many beatings (he even learned to romanticize the abuse as "the best thing that ever happened"), he lost his ability to identify with his son's pain. If he were to acknowledge his son's pain, then he would have to deal with his own. Bart was not only imitating his father's abuse, but also defending his actions by saying that he was helping his son grow up and get tough. Amazingly, he thought that he was doing his son a favor by inflicting severe emotional and physical pain on him!

Whether the form is physical, emotional, sexual, or some combination of the three, victims of child abuse experience profound emotional trauma. They do not know that such chronic pain is not a normal part of life (after all, they have nothing with which to compare it), and so they think that there is nothing they can do about it. Abuse severely undermines a child's sense of self-esteem, leaving the child feeling that he or she is completely without value. Because the child feels powerless and unvalued, the future is seen as unquestionably dark. There is no reason for any kind of optimism.

Thus, we see in the childhood victim the three elements of classic depression: helplessness, worthlessness, and hopelessness. Once these conditions are established, the child tends to take one of two basic psychological directions. One path is to fully experience the emotional pain. In this case, the child often grows up dealing with classic (feminine) symptoms: anxiety, phobia, depression, sexual disorders, or other problems based in this fearful childhood experience. The other path involves a "sealing over" of the emotional pain. Because feeling is so often associated with extreme pain, the child ceases to feel, and the emotions of these depressive experiences are converted into anger. They are then expressed indirectly, through schoolyard bullying, delinquent behavior, and sometimes through the abuse of others as an adult. Abused children who "seal over" their pain are at high risk for starting on the path to a lifetime of depression-based violence. The vast majority of those who do so are male.

We do not expect people who have been abused as children to grow up to be abusers because we assume that they know what it feels like to be abused. If one has empathy for the child, one never abuses him or her. But how can one have a sense of someone else's feeling if one has no sense of one's *own* feeling? Those victims that grow up to become abusers do so precisely because they no longer have an emotional awareness of what it feels like to be abused. The critical factor, then, in becoming an adult abuser is the sealing over of the emotional life. Such was the case for Bart. He kept his own pain sealed over by romanticizing it. This rationalization justified, for him, the abuse of his son. It is difficult for others to feel any sympathy for violent people because they cause such harm, and because their own pain is so obscure.

(It is important to note here that most people abused as children do NOT grow up to become abusers. We only use this for illustration because it is a risk factor. Note also that all adult perpetrators of abuse were not necessarily victims as children.)

How Is Dissociation from Feelings Related to Violent Behavior?

The stereotype of the schoolyard bully provides insight into the paradox of many depressed men who become violent. It may be that he feels worthless and angry, but he cannot face these feelings. The only way he can deal with these negative emotions is to seek out someone to dominate so that he can feel superior, if only for a moment. But his strategy results only in short-term gain. Nobody wants to be his friend because he is cruel, and he gets himself into trouble again and again. Not only is his behavior harmful to others, it is also self-defeating. Inside the bully is a little boy who wants to be valued and loved, but we may never get to see this little boy, or to come to like him. Over time, especially in the most severe cases, that little boy virtually ceases to exist, as his emotional life withers away and dies. His cruel behavior prevents him from getting the very things he so desires, but he cannot stop the cruelty because the ensuing vulnerability would be unbearable.

When expressed in this indirect manner, the behavioral expression of feelings is so distorted that the original emotions become unrecognizable, even to the person who is experiencing the feelings. Feeling threatened, he becomes hostile. Feeling dependent, he becomes overly independent or detached. Feeling sad, he becomes angry.

Should Men Be Excused from the Consequences of Violent and Destructive Behaviors Because They Are Depressed?

Absolutely not. Men's destructive behaviors hurt others, break laws, and are unconscionable. Clearly, social consequences precede understanding and treatment. There is no justification for violence in a family or anywhere else. However, we seek to prevent future generations from suffering through this legacy by designing effective treatments for today's fathers and husbands.

Men cannot and should not be excused from the consequences of their behavior. But to prevent and effectively treat violent behaviors, we must understand their origins and the paths by which they develop. We argue that men's violence begins behind the mask of masculine depression and that understanding, treating, and preventing this depression is one possible solution toward solving the problem of men's violence. There is no contradiction between striving to understand a perpetrator on the one hand and holding him responsible for his behavior on the other.

Why Can't Men Just Get Better on Their Own?

Because men's experience of depression tends to be distorted, solutions to their problems also tend to be distorted—and thus ineffective. Most of these strategies involve some attempt to distract and detach themselves from their negative feelings. Overwork, drinking, violence, sexual promiscuity, and power plays in their primary relationships are all attempts in this direction. These strategies are self-defeating, as they often make relationships, physical health, and other areas of a man's life worse. A kind of vicious cycle develops. A depressed man acts out self-destructively or insensitively to others, creating problems in living which, in turn, exacerbate his depressive feelings.

Even when depressed men are well aware of their problems, they are less likely to seek help in a culture that considers help seeking to be unmanly. Unable to express themselves, gain support from friends, or request professional help, many depressed men are left alone with their problems. All depressed men are disturbed, and, unfortunately, many also become disturbing. The solution is elusive because the appearance is deceiving.

What Happens to Men Who Grow Up Without Learning to Deal with Feelings and Inner Conflicts?

Adult men who fail to deal with emotional conflicts suffer themselves and/or cause others to suffer. The most severe cases involve homelessness, criminal behavior, and suicide. Consider the following statistics, all of which are related to the phenomenon of masculine depression:

- Of the over 1 million people in United States prisons, 90 percent are men.[18]
- 52 percent of all female murder victims in the United States are killed by their male partners or ex-partners.[19]
- 1.8 million women are victims of spousal abuse each year.[20]
- 70 percent of homeless people are men.[21]
- Men die an average of seven years earlier than women.
- Men are disproportionately involved in substance abuse.[22]

We can look at a variety of social and psychological forces that conspire to encourage men to deal with depression by becoming destructive to themselves and/or others. We will discuss these forces in depth in the next few chapters. They involve problematic childhood relationships with their mothers and fathers, the learning of poor techniques for dealing with emotional difficulties, and the failure of social systems to hold many men responsible for their destructive behavior. Even in relatively "normal" men, these conflicts can emerge when emotional pain combines with the cultural directives to "be a man."

In the larger culture, masculine depression is often seen as moral failure, mainly because of the harm to others that masculine depression usually breeds, and because men are considered to always be in control of themselves. Moreover, there is a sense that nothing can be done about disturbing male behavior. This "boys will be boys" attitude leaves people feeling helpless in addressing the problem. Because the pain behind the mask, the depressive origin of these behaviors, is not well understood, solutions are often punitive or misguided. Instead of looking at the origins of male behavior, people tend to focus solely on its harmful effects.

Why Is It Important to Identify These Problems As "Masculine Depression?"

The psychological literature on problem solving tells us that finding a useful solution to a problem depends critically on finding a useful *conceptualization* of that problem. We need helpful, action-oriented ways of thinking about a problem in order to solve it effectively. For example, seeing the American drug problem as a moral or criminal problem leads to one set of solutions (e.g., law enforcement strategies and moral education). However, if the same problem is viewed as a public health or economic inequality problem, an entirely different set of possible solutions are considered (e.g., job training, rehabilitation, preventive mental health services, even changes in tax law). In other words, new *descriptions* lead to new *prescriptions*. If one thinks about problematic male behaviors in traditional, "boys will be boys" fashion, then one becomes stuck in rather stale and unsuccessful strategies—punishing, ignoring, and moralizing about men with problems. Although it is important to hold people responsible for what they do, society must also find new ways of preventing harmful behaviors from occurring in the first place. Thus, we believe that men who commit crimes should go to jail, and that men who abuse their partners should lose that relationship and face criminal charges. Social standards of conduct come first. But we also want to help men understand and control their behavior so that they can prevent these problems from occurring in the first place. Many men need to develop different emotional skills so that they can live more fulfilling lives and have healthier relationships.

When Is Masculine Depression a Problem?

The answer to this question is simple—it is a problem when behaviors that are the expression of masculine depression affect the quality of a man's life and/or the quality of life for people who have to deal with him: his wife, children, co-workers, and friends. In other words, when a man's behavior is significantly disturbed or disturbing, everyone can benefit from some positive changes.

WHAT ARE THE SOLUTIONS TO MASCULINE DEPRESSION?

If the description of masculine depression fits you or someone you know, try not to be ashamed. As we will see in Chapter 2, masculine depression originates mainly in childhood, when you have very little control over what shapes your psychological style. It is courageous to confront masculine depression as a problem, and the good news is that you can begin to do something about it. The dilemma of masculine depression is not solely the fault of the man. It is, however, the man's responsibility to do something about it.

Having understood that a set of negative behaviors stems from this style of reacting to one's emotional pain, we are then in a position to prescribe ways in which men and their partners can solve problems associated with masculine depression. We believe that the problem can be approached from several angles. Men can act on their own in the healing process. Women can learn more about men's issues to help their partners. In a marriage or other primary relationship, a couple can work with each other to find new modes of interaction. Men can change their relationships with their close male friends in the direction of more emotional support.

Although we do not offer magical, "pop" psychology, oversimplified solutions to long-standing problems, we do believe that changes in individual and social definitions of masculinity are both possible and desirable. To undertake this process, people need to understand the familial, social, and unconscious origins of gender and depression. Most men know little about the effects of gender, having been raised to understand themselves as "generic human beings" rather than gendered people, and to understand women as exceptions or special cases. Moreover, men have learned to operate in the world by sets of rigid rules (many of which are learned in sports) that they think to be universal. When they enter relationships with women, men usually find out that women operate differently, and they are encouraged to believe that this difference exists because something is wrong with women! This misperception leads to competition (e.g., to not lose an argument), blaming (externalizing one's own failures), and isolation (the psychological and/or physical avoidance of the partner). As men begin to understand the processes by which they have come to think, feel, and behave in masculine ways (Part I of this book), they can also learn to appreciate other ways of operating in the world (Part II), and the results can be quite enriching. Men can learn to relate to women through intimacy rather than fear.

However, insight is not enough. Men need to recover the emotional lives they were forced to abandon, and this can be very difficult work. Some of it can be done by simply tuning in to one's everyday emotional experiences. But men also need to learn how to talk about their emotions in nonintellectualized ways, work to understand others' emotional experiences, and resist the urge to disconnect themselves from strong feelings. The process is slow and painstaking. After all, these feelings have been sealed over for years, and some men, because of their fear of vulnerability, might prefer that they remain sealed over. At the same time, the full experiencing of emotion is what connects the person to his most basic state of being. This kind of work can bring a vitality to a man's life that he never thought possible. We must learn as individuals, and as a culture, to deal with the problem of masculine depression. Failure to do so leaves us in a cycle of confusion, blaming, relationship difficulties, violence, and human suffering.

Chapter 2

Family Influences

We believe that the roots of masculine depression style are in the man's family of origin. What a boy learns about himself and about relationships with other people is very often different from what a girl learns, even when both are raised in the same family. We will demonstrate how boys experience unique mother-son relationships and unique father-son relationships, and how they begin to develop the defenses that they will later use in the gender socialization process. These experiences result in unnecessary and unnatural limitations in men's intimate relationships as adults. In this chapter, we will present a model for understanding the origins of masculine depression, beginning with a view of family development through a gender perspective.

WHAT ARE THE FAMILY ROOTS
OF MASCULINE DEPRESSION?

The manner in which a family functions affects the experience and development of each of its members. Healthy families most often produce healthy individuals. Families that function without consistent rules or realistic expectations more often produce individuals who have trouble negotiating relationships, the working world, and other adult demands. Families function as a result of the established relationships among individual members. The effect of these established relationships is easily recognized in divorced, blended, and single-parent families, where changing family roles and structures dramatically alter individuals' behaviors and identities. When a father is suddenly absent or a mother remarries, children often respond to this change with angry outbursts, sudden withdrawals, or other symptoms.

Parents (and the character of parents' relationships with each other) obviously have a profound effect on children by what they do or fail to do. Parents who are close and loving are apt to have more emotionally secure children than parents who fight and argue all of the time. Physically absent or emotionally unavailable parents clearly have as much of an impact on the development of children as parents who provide a caring and consistent relationship. It is one thing to have a loving mother and father, but quite another to have a loving mother and not feel close to one's father at all. The absent relationship has as much of a negative effect as the loving one has a positive effect. The need for a loving mother is met, while the need for a loving father goes unfulfilled.

The relationship with each parent is powerful whether the parent is positive or negative, active or absent. The absent parent, most often the father, affects both boys and girls, but in different ways. Girls may develop a distorted sense of what they can expect of men. If they enter intimate relationships with men as adults, their model of masculine inadequacy in relationships may cause problems. On the other hand, boys may fail to learn about very important aspects of masculine identity. Where there should be a male model for boys there is frequently a powerful and influential void. As we will see, this void can become one of the defining characteristics of problematic male development.

HOW ARE FAMILY RELATIONSHIPS STRUCTURED?

When family therapists try to get a "picture" of family dynamics they use diagrams similar to Figure 2.1 to illustrate relationships between family members. The top row of figures represents the parents; the bottom row represents the children.

The Emotional Relationships in a Family

Figure 2.1 presents an emotional picture of the family that may or may not be accurate. In this "typical" family, children are equally close to their parents, reflecting healthy generational boundaries between parents and children. The parents are also balanced in their relationship with each other and with their children. Notice that we put the word "typical" in quotations. Although we would like to think

FIGURE 2.1. The "Typical" Family Structure

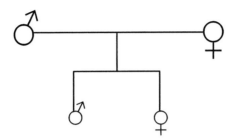

that families function in this manner, many do not. Equally shared functions and balanced relationships are idealized more than they are realized.

If we change the diagram to represent the truly typical emotional structure of the family, the balance looks different. One parent is often more psychologically and physically available to the children than the other parent. Who usually attends to children's most immediate and day-to-day needs? Who usually provides nurturing for children, takes them to piano lessons, picks them up from day care, or talks with them first about their troubles? In the traditional family, it is the mother. If we alter the diagram to represent the family's emotional structure, it would look more like Figure 2.2.

FIGURE 2.2. The Emotional Structure of a Family

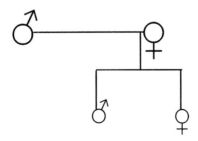

The Emotional and Power Relationships in a Family

In "The Emotional Structure" diagram, children are placed closer to the source of their emotional lives—their mother. For a variety of reasons, traditional fathers reveal less about themselves, are less attentive, and are less involved with their children's emotional lives than traditional mothers. In addition, the father's historical role as the family breadwinner has taken him away from the home much of the day. When both parents hold full-time jobs and work outside the home, the pattern of men's lesser domestic involvement (and the emotional distance that often goes with it) frequently continues—women still perform 75 percent of household and child care chores.[1] So, even in more modern households where both father and mother share the breadwinner role, traditional parental arrangements remain in evidence.

Families are also influenced by cultural patterns and expectations, and our culture is certainly not blind to gender. Men make more money than women and hold more upper-level positions. This pattern reflects an imbalance in the societal importance that is differentially attributed to men and women. Because it has been "a man's world," men often have had more economic and political power than women. How many families would hesitate to move to a new location for the father's new job? How many of the same families would think of moving for the mother's new job? By virtue of their gender, men have more political and economic power than women in this culture, a reflection of the longstanding tradition of patriarchy.

Now look at what happens if we include political and financial power in our diagram of a typical family (see Figure 2.3).

Power, Emotional, and Financial Relationships in a Family

Mainstream U. S. culture bestows men with dominance and privilege in the public sphere. At home, however, the effect of imbalanced political and financial power may be to further distance and isolate the typical father from the rest of the family. He frequently spends more time away from the home. His position in society may make him somewhat of an object of fear and an image of power

FIGURE 2.3. The Power Structure of a Family

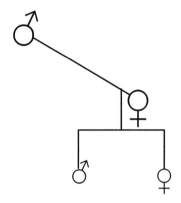

rather than of attachment. As father is less known and less connected to the emotional life of the family, he needs to be more
self-contained and self-sufficient. Although other family members
may see him as powerful and angry, he may feel alone, frustrated,
and powerless. In the world he might be referred to as "the man of
the house," make more money, achieve more success, and gain
acclaim through promotions and awards. At home, however, he
may feel emotionally unconnected and isolated from intimacy.

A Father's Isolation in a Family

The poorer and less developed a father's relationships are within the
family, the more emotionally isolated he feels. This experience of
isolation causes stress in relationships throughout the family. If we add
the marital and family stresses that result from the emotional, political,
and financial structure of the family, the father (in addition to being
more distant) becomes less connected as well (see Figure 2.4).

Under these conditions, marriages are frequently strained. In addition to the usual stresses of living, family members feel the stress from
unbalanced relationships and unequal family roles. When a mother is
overwhelmed by the tasks of maintaining the family and household
chores on her own, the entire family feels it. The effects of the isola-

FIGURE 2.4. A Father's Isolation in a Family

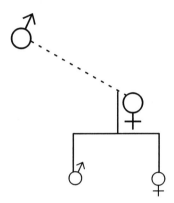

tion, frustration, and emotional powerlessness that fathers frequently feel are just as profound. However, fathers are not seen as the emotional centers of families. Typically, a father's value and contribution to a traditional family is what he can do for others more than how he feels or helps others feel. It is sometimes easy to overlook a father's isolation and its subsequent effect on all family members.

HOW DOES FAMILY STRUCTURE INFLUENCE A BOY'S DEVELOPMENT?

In a family where there is an imbalance in the power structure, the son does not know his father well. Too often, he only sees his father's stinging temper, produced by an isolation and stress that is neither revealed nor understood. As he gets blamed or shamed for failures, mistakes, and other ways in which he lets his father down, the son personalizes his father's anger. Instead of seeing a man who works out problems intimately with his wife, he experiences a man who tends to blame her for all of their problems, keeping her at arm's length and intimidating her. He sees a man who never talks to anyone about his feelings and conflicts nor asks for help.

Instead, he sees a man who seeks power compulsively and acts in ways that are at times dangerous and mean spirited.

Since the boy does not feel this same power inside of himself, he experiences himself as being very different from his father. While daughters tend to be closer to their mothers and to have an experience of female similarities, boys tend to experience a primary and *unnamed difference* between themselves and their primary adult male role models. Boys do not have what their fathers appear to have. Despite being emotionally isolated in the family, fathers appear to be powerful and strong. Boys may feel inadequate when they compare themselves to these men.

To appear masculine, boys must develop those qualities that fathers seem to have: rugged independence, dominance, self-confidence, and restricted emotionality. These characteristics are some of the extreme aspects of masculinity. Yet the extreme becomes the norm and, sadly, a boy's first model of masculinity is often based on the exaggerated behaviors of a man who is emotionally isolated from his family. In order to keep their masculine identities intact, boys gradually lose awareness of any sense of personal inadequacy and take on the habit of masculine posturing. Because his father does not display any evidence of self-doubt, the boy unconsciously learns that feelings and (especially) displays of inadequacy are indications of a lack of masculinity. Any feelings of vulnerability, sadness, or hurt are similarly seen as evidence of masculine weakness. To further complicate the picture, boys cannot name or talk about this conflict. Acknowledging or asking for help with self-doubt is considered unmanly. Doing so would threaten the masculinity they have learned to value so highly. Losing awareness of these feelings becomes a valuable coping skill. A boy learns how to "act like a man," to avoid losing at all costs, and to not tolerate making mistakes. He defends himself against anyone who thinks that he is not powerful, strong, or forever right. The son grows into the man that his father appeared to be. When he grows up and marries, he wants and needs emotional closeness with his wife but is terrified of intimacy, so he settles for what he knows how to do: compete, detach, bully, and act in other stereotypical and unhealthy masculine ways. To a great extent, he becomes his father, shaped as much by his fears as by his strengths.

HOW DO PEER GROUPS INFLUENCE
FAMILY DYNAMICS?

Little boys who come from families with unbalanced power struc-tures go to school and begin a very significant gender socialization process. As boys talk and play with other boys and with adults who hold stereotypical expectations for males' behaviors, the socializa-tion process strengthens the unhealthy masculine defenses and ways of relating that were learned at home. Gender socialization encour-ages boys to hide their real human needs in the service of appearing to be masculine and self-assured. For instance, boys learn that they lose the approval of peers if they display their emotional pain, so they learn to respond to shame by fighting and posturing with their peers. They learn that task and image are always more important than feeling and experience, so they erect strong psychological defenses against "dangerous" feelings. The stakes are high. In an effort to protect the very essence of his identity, a boy often surrenders to a false sense of self. As we will see in Chapter 3, the rigid limitations of traditional masculinity provide boys with a measure of safety from the social punishment that is exacted for expressions of "feminine" (vulnerable) emotions.

Over time, these defenses become a core part of the boy's person-ality. The gender socialization process that takes place when a boy interacts with male peers in his neighborhood and school is crucial in continuing the avoidance of vulnerable feelings. A boy learns to "act like a man" and deny a full range of emotional expression. He engages socially with other "defended" boys. The result is illus-trated in Figure 2.5.

This process continues throughout school. Noted family therapist Frank Pittman describes the way that boys internalize male peer groups as an "invisible male chorus" that establishes and enforces a set of norms: toughness, self-reliance, antifemininity, homophobia, competi-tiveness, and fearlessness.[2] This *locker room chorus* is supported and substantiated by concrete interactions that are "remembered" in the unconscious. The overall theme is constant: always defend against vulnerability.

Men take the locker room chorus and the family structure with them as they enter adult life and marry. How can an intimate relationship with a mate proceed, given these profoundly negative influences?

FIGURE 2.5. The Male Peer Group Socialization Process

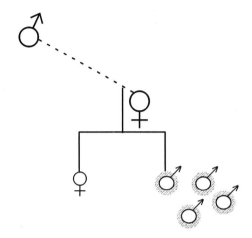

HOW DO NEGATIVE MASCULINE CHILDHOOD EXPERIENCES LEAD TO RELATIONSHIP PROBLEMS IN ADULTHOOD?

The difficulties experienced by men in relationships are predict-able and well documented. We are all familiar with the usual "marital dance" (she pursues, he distances), as well as the emo-tional isolation men experience in families, as illustrated earlier. Then there are the affairs and alcohol abuse that are the ways that many men disguise their feelings of depression and shame. And finally, there is the most detrimental effect of all: the domestic violence and child abuse that often results when men cannot toler-ate fears or weaknesses in themselves and, consequently, in those whom they love. The hypermasculine, or "macho" coping style hides a man's inadequately developed and anxiety-filled feelings about himself. Unfortunately, this dysfunctional style of coping is often passed down from father to son, as illustrated in Figure 2.6.

FIGURE 2.6. Intergenerational Transmission of the Masculine Dilemma

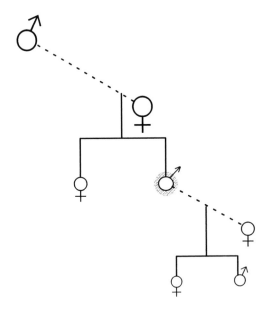

Men and women meet, fall in love, and marry. The relationship that develops depends on each person's willingness to share and be vulnerable with the other person in an emotional way. Unfortunately, he has learned to avoid "sharing himself" and all of that other "feminine stuff"—the stuff that relationships are made of. The following story illustrates the processes we have described:

> Mike appeared to be the American success story. He had emigrated to the United States eleven years ago with a minimal mastery of the language and a strong work ethic. Over the years, he had worked his way up to a managerial position, and he ran his store quite successfully. Everyone who met him came away with respect for his work and honesty as well as praise for the way that he treated people. His wife would frequently hear how lucky she was to have such a wonderful man. But it was clear that all was not well. Mike came to therapy when his wife took both children, moved out, obtained a restraining order, and initiated the divorce process.

In the initial therapy session, Mike expressed a willingness to work on the problems that contributed to the failure of the marriage. He said that he was plagued by feelings of fear and insecurity. He described a daily struggle with a deep sense of inadequacy and an accompanying desire to withdraw from everything. His accomplishments had not come easily. Every day was another struggle with fear, anxiety, and concerns about being successful. He *appeared* successful (and he was in many ways), but he felt a range of complex and intense feelings that he had never shared with anyone. Mike was now able to talk about the emotional isolation he had always experienced. It was worse now that his wife had left and he had to come home every day to an empty house. He spoke of both a dislike and a fear of being alone, and he doubted that he could handle the experience of spending time by himself.

Mike had tried to rule the house like a benevolent dictator, yet his wife saw the house as her domain. Thus, their relationship became a perpetual struggle for power. When they fought, he felt that he was simply right, that there would be no compromise, and that it was unmanly to back down, especially from a woman. His wife was strong-willed, and so Mike used verbal and physical abuse to intimidate her. In therapy, he admitted that he knew that these tactics were wrong and that he felt shame and remorse. However, he also found it impossible to alter his dictatorial stance. He never thought of his wife as an equal, only as a confusing creature who needed to be controlled. On the inside, Mike felt worthless, fearful, vulnerable, and alone. On the outside, he looked impenetrable, angry, and dangerous.

Although many men master several aspects of adult life, including job advancement, money management, and mechanical skills, they often have a great deal of difficulty dealing with the everyday challenges of relationships. While most traditional working environments operate on masculine principles (don't feel, shut up and get the job done), relationships fail on these same principles. Men can master the working world, but too frequently they fail at home. Men can also succeed at home—but in order to do so they need to know how to develop relationship skills, a task we will take up in the later chapters of this book. We now turn to an in-depth discussion of three profound influences in a boy's life: his mother, his father, and his peers. Negative experiences in any of these relationships can trigger the beginnings of masculine depression.

HOW DOES A PROBLEMATIC MOTHER-SON RELATIONSHIP CONTRIBUTE TO MASCULINE DEPRESSION?

Unlike girls, boys are predominantly raised by a person of the other sex. Thus, while girls tend to experience themselves in terms of *attachment* to a same-sex person, boys tend to experience themselves in terms of *detachment* from someone whom they experience as different from themselves in an important way. Analytic psychologist Nancy Chodorow described basic masculine identity as that of being "not mother."[3] Girls learn, "I am what Mom is." One would think that boys would learn, "I am what Dad is," but typically, boys learn, "I am what Mom is *not*," because they spend so much more time with their mothers and because their fathers are usually not emotionally or physically available as role models. In contemporary times, even when children are cared for by someone other than their mothers, that someone is most often female, as it is rare for child care personnel to be male. Thus, the early psychological identity of males is based on the negative "what I am not," and masculinity is experienced as "not feminine." The boy has to negate the feminine in himself and deny himself the comfort and relational skills that his mother offers in order to be "not mother."

The implications of this negative sense of identity and rejection of the feminine are substantial. A sense of self based on *not* being like someone is less clear and more defensive than one based on a model that is seen and heard each day. How would one know if he was successfully being "not mother?" There is no way to affirm a negative, and boys can never be absolutely sure, once and for all, that they are "not mother." Fathers who are inaccessible provide another source of the son's doubts about his adequacy. Seeds of anxiety and insecurity are sown in the boy's unconscious. He cannot be like his adult male model and can never fully be unlike his female caregiver. He has to negate the feminine in himself and deny himself the comfort and relational skills that his mother offers in order to define himself as "not mother."

These conflicting childhood feelings in boys can be confusing and seem unresolvable. Later, behaviors are produced that look completely different from the original conflict, just as an oak tree looks completely different from an acorn. The aggressive and avoidant behavior of an adult male in a problematic intimate relationship looks completely different from the vulnerable feelings of a boy trying to understand being male while he is being raised by a female. But the behavior is rooted in the feeling.

A boy who gets too close to his mother is likely to be shamed as a "mama's boy." On the other hand, he cannot get too far away from her or he will feel unconnected, lonely, and afraid. After all, it is a woman (usually mom) who provides for the boy's most basic physical and emotional needs. Thus, boys experience a seemingly unresolvable dilemma. They must remain "not too close, not too far away." This theme of masculine depression begins in childhood and is repeated in later intimate relationships with women, as men tend to feel uncomfortable being too attached or too detached. Mother (and later, intimate partner) is both feared and desired at the same time.

We sometimes hear men say of women, "Can't live with 'em; can't live without 'em." This difficulty in heterosexual relationships is a recapitulation of the basic dilemma of a boy's problematic relationship with his mother, especially when there is no corresponding warm relationship with his father. This defensive disidentification with the mother is not inevitable, natural, or desirable. Boys can gain a great deal from their relationship with their mothers. They lose a great deal by disidentifying with her and failing to take on her positive characteristics. For many boys, these characteristics are those that can help them in the worlds of relationships and feelings.

The reality is that the boy needs his mother's love. He needs to learn relationship skills, nurturance, tolerance, and an understanding of feelings from her, but his defensive gender identity can prevent him from doing so. Adult men must unlearn their defenses and revalue these intimacy skills, rather than seeing them as a threat to their masculinity.

Masculine depression is strongly rooted in this relationship struggle. Perhaps the best way to get this point across is by way of contrast.

Because a girl is the same sex as her mother, a girl's psychological identity is less ambivalent. She can have an adult model to be close to and imitate, without risking engulfment (being "swallowed up" emotionally) or alienation (becoming an outcast). Thus, issues of healthy separation may be more problematic for adult women than for men. (This is not to say that it *should* be this way, but that it often is.) By contrast, adult males tend to have fewer problems separating (at least on the surface) from women in order to establish their identities. They did this as young boys, when they realized they were "not mother." Just as boys need to be close to their mothers, adult males need to be close to their partners, but the fear of engulfment can create attachment problems for males.

For most men, the conflict of "not too close, not too far away" becomes unconscious. In contrast to the conscious, the unconscious is the part of the mind that does not know time and does not know individual differences. The unconscious mind's fear of engulfment and alienation becomes activated in an intimate relationship with a woman. In the unconscious, there is no distinction between the mother and the wife. Primal, powerful fears of rejection and conflict are reactivated in an intimate adult relationship with a woman.

While of all this may sound too psychoanalytic (or even a little far-fetched), the bottom line is that males simply experience a basic undercurrent of anxiety regarding distance and closeness in an important relationship with a female. Men are ambivalent. They want both, but both distance and closeness are experienced as threats, and so they often dance between the extremes of each. In reality, they can have (and they need) both individual identity and intimacy, just as women do.

The emotional experience of men in an intimate relationship produces a discomfort that few men can identify or understand. Just as it is hard to solve a problem that you cannot name, men have difficulty learning how to deal with their mixed feelings about relationships with women. Many men will "act out" their anxieties, for instance, by isolating themselves, treating their wives cruelly, or having extramarital affairs. A direct connection develops between the way boys experience themselves in relation to their mothers and the way men experience themselves in intimate relationships with adult women. John's story shows us this process:

John had an advanced degree in biochemistry and was an important person at work. He had a great deal of responsibility and worried about various projects all day long. At home, he was unresponsive to his wife's expectations for help and cooperation with all of the tasks involved in raising three children and maintaining a household. In John's childhood, his mother was a tyrant compared with his easygoing and deferent father. It had always made him uncomfortable to see his mother's anger and his father's avoidance. As a boy, he was frightened and intimidated by his mother. He felt the same way whenever his wife got angry, but he also had learned the cultural message that men should dominate their wives. When his wife raised her voice, he responded by flying into a rage. She usually reacted by backing down but began to develop long-standing feelings of resentment and frustration at John's behavior.

John's therapist asked him why he responded to his wife with such rage. He looked incredulous, as if the answer was more than obvious. He answered, "She was ANGRY!" as if that statement explained it all. Clearly, he thought there was no possible response (or feeling) except for rage. He had no idea that, directly preceding his rage, he felt intimidated and threatened by his wife. He was not aware of these feelings because he had learned the golden gender rule about not acknowledging any feelings except for anger. Unconsciously he acted as if his wife's anger was as dangerous and intimidating as his mother's. His reaction was to defend himself from the fear that he felt when his mother was angry. He could not hear what his wife was concerned about. He could only react to her potential anger and the discomfort that it might cause.

This basic relational conflict in male development results in unnamed and unresolved feelings toward women. Men have basic needs for intimacy and emotional expression that remain unrecognized, even to themselves. Thus these needs are rarely fulfilled. Over time, feelings are "forgotten"—*dissociated* from conscious awareness—and later acted out in the context of relationship problems.

HOW DOES A PROBLEMATIC
FATHER-SON RELATIONSHIP CONTRIBUTE
TO MASCULINE DEPRESSION?

Whether by their presence or absence, fathers are profoundly important to the psychological development of sons. All too often, the father is physically and/or emotionally missing in his son's life. Thus, the son is deprived of the experience of intimacy with his father. Not knowing how an adult male functions, facing successes, defeats, fear, anger, etc., a boy must guess. His guesses are guided by the myths that surround adult masculinity. His father is seen as a larger-than-life hero who masters the world effortlessly and fearlessly. As a result, the boy grows up with a sense of inadequacy, a feeling that he can never measure up to the mythical masculine ideal. The truth is, no one can. This feeling of inadequacy is based in shame. Gender demands prevent him from directly comparing his experience with that of other men. He can only do so indirectly—by comparing his inner feelings to men's outward appearance. When he does so, he comes up short. He can never feel as confident and autonomous on the inside as adult males appear on the outside.

Young boys logically assume that appearance is reality. Since they do not have access to the inner fears, sadness, or sentimentality of men, they presume that these things do not exist. The problem is that the boy sees the finished product of the socialization process, a masculine appearance, in the adult male. When he compares his own inner experience, which is clouded in childhood fears and inadequacies, to a fully developed and psychologically defended man, he concludes "I am not that . . . I cannot measure up." While the initial experience of the relationship with the mother is based on *fear*—fear of being too close or too far away, the experience of self in relationship to the father is one of *inadequacy*—"I can never be as confident or as strong as that; there must be something very wrong with me if I feel this scared and unsure of myself." This conflict becomes dissociated (separated from conscious thought and feeling) over time, so that it is not experienced emotionally or felt in any direct way. Rather, it is acted out in behaviors harmful to the self and others. Some theorists have referred to the "father wound,"[4] a void which exists in men due to lack of a relationship with their fathers.

This psychological issue becomes a central part of masculine depression and its accompanying destructive behaviors. The man desperately needs to prove to himself and the world that he is adequate, but he cannot do so until he acknowledges to himself that he sometimes feels unsure of himself.

The outward behavior of men frequently does not reflect their feelings, and this discrepancy is what masculine depression is all about. Depression is the chronic experience of unmet needs. Because of the constrictions brought by cultural messages about masculinity, men show their feelings in disguised form, and these feelings remain mostly unrecognized, unexpressed, and misunderstood by self and others. The original confusing feelings boys experience in the relationships with their mothers and fathers manifest themselves in adulthood as unmet needs for security, confidence, and mastery. Men show their feelings in disguised form and, because they are disguised, the underlying needs can never be met. It is with this inner conflict that boys enter the masculine socialization process.

HOW DOES PEER SOCIALIZATION LEAD TO MASCULINE DEPRESSION?

The third influence upon male development is the socialization process in which boys develop definitions about acceptable ways to handle emotional, social, and practical situations in the world. When dealing with relationships, boys learn a distinctly masculine style of negotiating a variety of problems without revealing their feelings. Masculine social norms place high values on competitiveness, aggressiveness, and toughness. Emotional expressions are shamed and stamped out as unacceptable for males. For example, a boy learns early in his life that crying in public (or admitting that he cries in private) will result in his being ostracized from his male peer group. As an adult, he continues to carry the sense that it is dangerous to feel too much.

Thus, traditional masculinity is the end product of the male socialization process. It is a style of interacting in the world that enables one to stress autonomy, independence, competitiveness, and aggressiveness at the expense of revealing feelings and working through fears and perceived inadequacies in important relationships.

But feelings cry for expression, and the denial of painful emotional conflicts contributes to physical disorders (such as back pain, heart disease, and ulcers) as well as to behaviors that defy reason, such as avoiding or abusing loved ones.

The overall effect of masculine socialization is to reinforce the dissociative process that begins in the boy's relationship with his parents. The most extreme way to deal with pain and uncertainty is to adopt the hypermasculine, or "macho man" image. The man who does so becomes adept at shutting down his feelings and appearing to be more like a machine than a human being. But maintaining this image exacts a huge price. The more that feelings are dissociated and therefore unconscious, the more dangerous to self (health) and others (relationships) the resulting behaviors become.

The dilemma men experience in relationships and the demand for emotional denial are at the core of masculine depression. Adult men learn to live by the relationship rules that began with family structure and were reinforced by cultural demands. When men are stripped of their basic humanity, they behave in inhuman ways, most often in the most private and important part of their lives, their intimate relationships.

HOW CAN MEN DEVELOP "HEALTHY" (AS OPPOSED TO "TRADITIONAL") MASCULINITY?

The unhealthy outcome of male socialization that we have described is not inevitable. In the healthy family, a young boy has the experience of equal access to equal parents. He learns that Mom and Dad compromise and negotiate differences in a fair and respectful manner. Both parents perform a variety of parenting tasks: cooking, household chores, discipline, problem solving, nurturing, and money management. The boy learns that fathers are powerful but not frightening, and that they use their strength to build, not destroy. He learns that being close to a woman is comforting and enriching, not emasculating. He learns to trust people and cooperate by watching both his mother and father. The son begins to learn about himself by utilizing his father as an active and understandable guide. He learns to tolerate frustrations or temporary failures as a part of the process of learning and improving. He is not afraid to make or admit to mistakes, which he comes to see as part of the learning process rather than as a shameful part of the self. He learns that men and women join together as cooperative partners, not as adversaries. Because he does not have a core of shame and insecurity, he feels free to express himself, explore his unique potential, and find his place in the world.

All of these experiences help men to develop healthy masculinity. As we will see in Chapters 5 and 6, healthy masculinity begins with healthy relationships, both with the self and with other men. When men reconnect with unrecognized and unexpressed feelings within themselves, and when these feelings are accepted by other men, the traditional limitations of masculinity give way to healthy and full expressions of masculinity. Masculinity is then restored as an expression of humanity.

Chapter 3

Inhumane Treatment
Leads to Inhuman Behavior:
The Socialization Process

If you want to learn something about how boys become men, ask adult males to describe childhood messages they received about masculinity. In our experience, men have little difficulty in recalling at least a few stories of defining moments when they learned what "being a man" means. These defining moments are an important part of learning complex social and emotional ways of being. They contain messages that guide males through later life events—telling them what to do, how to act, what is expected of them, and what they should expect of others. The following stories are examples of childhood episodes that highlight the powerful influence of masculine socialization on a boy's behavior and his sense of self. Listen for the messages embedded in the following childhood experiences:

> When my grandfather would visit, he would grab me and squeeze me in his arms until it hurt. I would scream and cry—that seemed to make it worse, because everyone would laugh at me.

> *   *   *

> Some neighborhood kids wouldn't let me have my wagon back, and it was time to go home. My dad met me at the door as I was crying about what they had done to me. He refused to let me in the house until I brought my wagon back. I found those kids, and I punched the biggest one right in the mouth. The others ran away, and I took my wagon home to the glowing approval of my father.

*   *   *

In every movie I saw as a kid, the guy who beat up the most people always got the girl.

*   *   *

I was terrible at shop class. I kind of wanted to learn how to cook, but I kept that to myself, because I knew that my male friends would laugh at me if I told them.

*   *   *

I have a brother who was only about a year younger than I. When we misbehaved as children, my father used to whip us with his belt, and we always cried. One time, my brother decided that, no matter how much it hurt, he wasn't going to cry. After he had been whipped, my father told me how great that was that my brother could control himself like that. He told me I should be more like my brother.

*   *   *

When it was snack time in kindergarten, one child would be chosen to go down the hall and bring the milk back in a red wagon. It was always a boy. The girls always wanted to do it, but they were never allowed.

*   *   *

I loved watching football on TV when I was young. The first time I played tackle football, I learned that football really hurts! It makes sense to me now—if a big guy runs as fast as he can and knocks you down, it's going to be painful. But it had never occurred to me that those pro football players were probably in pain almost every play. When I went to high school, I figured out why they did it. Even the ugliest, stupidest football player had a girlfriend. I was on the track team. No girls were interested in me.

*   *   *

I'll never forget Halloween in the first grade. We were supposed to come to school in costume, and my mother thought it would be cute to dress me up as a girl. I didn't really want to do it, but I went along with it anyway. It was the most humiliating day of my life. The other kids teased me until I cried.

These stories illustrate what is well-known to gender psychologists—that males and females are subject to different and rather sharply defined expectations for behavior. Each story contains the same basic theme. They all convey to the boy that, to be considered masculine and worthwhile, he must deny and repress a natural response (such as avoiding pain, expressing vulnerable feelings, gravitating toward certain interests and activities, or seeing females as equals) and replace it with a "masculine" response (such as submitting to pain, suppressing emotional responses, having only those interests that are socially defined as gender-appropriate, or viewing females as less capable and valuable than males). These inhumane treatments teach children to behave in less than fully human ways. And, although we have presented defining childhood moments for purposes of illustrating gender messages, one should be aware that gender socialization is a daily event, not only in the life of a child, but also in the everyday experiences of adults. The gender socialization process is powerful, (sometimes) subtle, and pervasive. All too often, we learn how we are expected to behave before we learn whom we want to be. Gender messages are important sources of how to behave.

WHAT ARE GENDER MESSAGES?

A gender message is any piece of information (verbal or nonverbal; direct or indirect) that communicates the expectation that males and females should (and a belief that they do) behave differently, experience themselves differently, and experience the world differently. These messages convey the cultural expectation that the person will take his or her place in an established social structure defined in large part by gender. These social expectations frequently maintain cultural consistency at the expense of individual expression. Gender messages are one aspect of the larger socialization process that introduces children to a world in which their culture organizes ways of thinking, labels experiences, and assigns values to people, things, behaviors, and ideas.

As psychologist Sandra Bem points out, "The kinds of human beings that children and adults become depend on their daily social experiences; and these social experiences are, in turn, preprogrammed by institutionalized social practices. . . . This simultaneous transmission and pickup of information is initiated every time the active, pattern-seeking child is exposed to a culturally significant social practice."[1] The person is encouraged to take on the worldview of a culture (which Bem refers to as a cultural "lens") a daily basis. More often than not, this "lens" is transferred *nonconsciously*. In other words, it becomes a set of unarticulated, unexamined, and implicit set of assumptions by which people live their lives. In mainstream U.S. culture, these assumptions include the belief that males and females are essentially and categorically different from each other, that everyone should be heterosexual, that males are "naturally" unemotional, aggressive, and interpersonally distant, and that females are "naturally" emotional, nurturing, and oriented toward people. Relatively few people question these assumptions, and so most people tend to live out these expectations with little awareness that they have the option to behave differently from prescribed gender roles.

Gender messages literally begin at birth. They are communicated by various aspects of culture: peer groups, parents, television, movies, books, and political figures, to name a few. These gender standards are enforced by rewards, punishments, and access to "masculine" or "feminine" places such as the kitchen, the repair shop, the fishing hole, and certain sports venues.

What Roles Do Gender Messages Play in a Child's Behavior and Sense of Self?

Gender messages mainly serve to restrict children by forcing them to see themselves in certain ways and to act accordingly. Compared with boys who like contact sports or girls who like to sew, emotional boys or ambitious girls have to struggle more to express themselves. They may suffer from lowered self-confidence and self-esteem, based on rejection and disapproval by important people in their lives and the culture in general. There exists a kind of cultural conspiracy, some of it conscious and some of it unconscious, to steer people into narrow gender roles. Generally, the result is a restriction of our development and our ability to fully realize and express our potentials.

Enlightened parents realize that this rigid gendering is not beneficial to their children's development, and they sometimes endeavor to provide a "gender neutral" environment. This task turns out to be more difficult than it appears for two reasons. First, mothers and fathers tend to model different behaviors in the home (many of which fit cultural gender stereotypes), and children tend to imitate these behaviors. Second, the gender neutral environment all but disappears as soon as one turns on the television or sends the child out to play with his or her same-sex peer group. Gender messages are strongly embedded in many aspects of daily experience, not just in parent-child interactions. Nonetheless, parents who are aware of gender demands, and who help their children understand these demands are giving their children important tools with which to negotiate their ways in the world.

At What Point in a Child's Life Do Gender Influences Begin to Have an Effect?

According to some research evidence, the answer to this question is, "within twenty-four hours of birth." In one classic psychological study, parents were asked to describe babies who were less than one day old. Newborn girls were described as softer, finer, and smaller. Boys were described as larger, stronger, more alert, and hardier. Several measurements of the infants, including height, weight, muscle tone, and respiration rates indicated no objective basis for making these distinctions.[2] Certainly the people describing these infants were unaware that their perceptions were biased so strongly by their gender assumptions. Nonetheless, they were profoundly influenced by their gender expectations and passed them along without knowing it.

A similar study gives us a clue to how these distorted perceptions serve to influence the social worlds of girls and boys. In this
study, mothers were asked to play with a six-month-old baby. For
some of the mothers, the baby was called "Adam" and was
dressed in blue pants. For others, the *same baby* was dressed in a
pink dress and called "Beth." Those who thought they were playing with a boy usually offered him a toy train. The ones who
played with "Beth" usually offered dolls. They also tended to hold
the child more closely and describe "her" in gender-stereotyped
ways (actually, the child was male).[3]

In interviews, these mothers all said that boys and girls were no
different at this age and should be treated in exactly the same ways.
Thus, the sex-typed behaviors and judgments that occurred were
apparently completely unconscious and based solely on the gender
label and dress of the child. In case you are wondering whether
fathers would have acted similarly to these mothers, a good deal of
research evidence supports that adult males are even more stereotypical in their perceptions than adult females.[4]

The major negative effect of stereotyping is that it influences a
person to see a *category* or *label* (in this case, male or female)
before he or she sees an individual. In response to these largely
unconscious gender perceptions, parents (and other socializing
agents) often put boys and girls into different social and physical
environments, communicate different expectations for their behavior, and reward or punish them for different actions. As we will see
later, this socialization continues to be present in the lives of adult
men and women.

What Evidence Supports the Power
of Gender Messages for Children?

Numerous studies demonstrate the power of social norms. In a
very interesting one, children were asked to rate the relative
"wrongness" of behaviors in four domains: moral (e.g., pushing
another child off of a swing), conventional (e.g., eating a cookie in
class when it is against the rules), personal (e.g., staying inside
when the weather is nice), and gender (e.g., a boy wearing nail
polish or a girl having a crew cut). Kindergarten and eighth graders
rated the gender "violations" as *worse* than physically hurting

another child! Interestingly, third- and fifth-graders rated gender transgressions as the least problematic of the four. Why children become less concerned with stereotypes in middle childhood is anybody's guess, but it is clear that, by the time they become teenagers, children recapture the sense of rigid gendering they had in early childhood. These were normal children, responding in a way that reflected the social norms they had learned. They judged the adherence to gender role norms as even more important than the avoidance of violent behaviors.[5]

WHAT DIFFERENCES ARE FOUND
IN THE PHYSICAL AND SOCIAL ENVIRONMENTS
OF MALES AND FEMALES?

Imagine that you are visiting the house of some friends who are the parents of an eight-year-old boy. Shortly after you arrive, the boy tells you that he wants to show you his room, so you walk upstairs with him as he proudly opens the bedroom door.

What do you expect to see? Certainly not dolls, ruffles, pastel colors, or floral decorations. Boys' rooms contain far more sports equipment, animal furnishings, and transportation toys than girls' rooms. If you play with the boy, are you more likely to "horse around" or to have a make-believe tea party? If you talk to him about growing up, are you more likely to ask him about his future career or about his plans to become a parent? When he is old enough to take on some household chores, will he be cutting the grass or babysitting? When he goes out to play in his single-sex peer group, will the interactions he has with his male friends have a different character than that of his sister's peer group? What gender typed images is he likely to see on television?

We could go on and on with these questions, and the answers to all of them are obvious. In many important ways, boys and girls grow up in distinctly different worlds. Socializing agents make male-female distinctions in the kind of decor one is supposed to enjoy, the kinds of work one is supposed to do, the kinds of colors one is supposed to like, the kinds of hobbies one is supposed to have, and a wide variety of other experiences and behaviors.

WHAT ARE THE MAJOR SEX DIFFERENCES IN CHILDHOOD GENDER SOCIALIZATION?

A growing body of research helps us to describe differences in gender socialization and the implications of these differences:

Male Children Are Held Less Often Than Female Children

Why we see this difference is anybody's guess, but there seems to be a pervasive sense that boys don't need to be held and cuddled as much as girls do.[6] Perhaps parents unconsciously fear that doing so will compromise boys' independence or "feminize" them. Classic research indicates that physical contact in early childhood is the basis for attachment to the parent and, later, for the ability to cope with one's fears.[7] Frequent childhood physical contact has positive effects in several areas of psychological development.[8] Basic physical deprivation may have implications for later problems some males have in getting close to others and understanding others' feelings.

Boys Are Handled More Vigorously Than Girls

Fathers, especially, seem to think it important to toss children around, particularly boys.[9] Although this experience may contribute to the boy's later awareness of his body in space, it is also reflective of the notion that males can and should be able to "take it" more. It also provides a very early expectation that boys will live in a more physical world and girls in a more relational world. Girls are more apt to play out family themes through relational tea parties and interactions among doll house characters.

Boys' Chores and Activities Take Them Farther Away from the Place of Residence Than Do Girls' Chores and Activities

Boys are much more likely than girls to find themselves in the yard, garage, or down the street.[10] On the positive side, these environments encourage boys to explore and discover the world. On the negative side, we see the beginning of the definition of the domestic world as the world of the feminine. Boys' activities usually put them in settings where problem solving and dealing with *things* are emphasized, rather than emotional coping and dealing with *people*. As the great developmental psychologist Jeanne Block put it, we give girls "roots" and give boys "wings."[11]

Boys' and Girls' Peer Groups Differ Markedly

Boys' groups tend to emphasize competition, aggression, and self-assertion, and boys are expected to dominate and fight with each other. They tend not to emphasize affiliation or cooperation to the degree that girls' groups do. Relationships are usually defined as less important than tasks.[12] When there are disputes in games, girls tend to attempt to resolve the conflict to the satisfaction of all. In boys' groups, the goal is usually to correctly interpret the rule regardless of how anybody feels about it. In fact, boys sometimes spend an entire play time arguing about the rules and never getting around to playing the game. When somebody gets hurt in a girls' game, the game is usually over. In boys' games, there is an effort to get the person out of the playing area so that the game, which is defined as more important than the person, can continue. (This arrangement obviously continues into school, college, and professional sports as well). An injured boy often has to walk home or to a teacher in order to attend to the injury.

In many childhood (as well as adult) environments, males find themselves in situations that call for dealing with the unfamiliar, discovering the physical world, and ignoring or suppressing both the emotional life and the experience of being attached to another person. We tend to give males very little practice in taking care of another human being, thinking about someone else's emotional experience, or weighing the relative merits of task and relationship. Yet we expect men to marry and be intimate in adulthood despite the behavioral and personality deficits that are systematically introduced throughout his early life. Inhumane treatment leads to inhuman behavior.

WHAT ROLE DOES REWARD AND PUNISHMENT PLAY IN GENDER STEREOTYPING?

In a stereotypical situation, a little boy is hurt and feels like crying. As his father sees his son's eyes begin to well up with tears, he says threateningly, "*I'll* give you something to cry about." The message is clear—if you don't keep your hurt feelings to yourself, you may well suffer more pain. This pain may be direct, as in the above example, or it may take the form of disapproval or interpersonal distancing from a parent, playmate, or other important person. A parent's disappointment in a child is a powerful motivator for the child to act and experience the self differently.

There are not many "laws" in psychology, but one, the "law of effect," was first proposed by E. L. Thorndike. It states that behaviors followed by pleasant circumstances tend to increase in frequency, while those followed by unpleasant circumstances tend to decrease in frequency.[13] Plain, simple, and obvious: follow a behavior with reward, and you are much more likely to see it again. Follow it with punishment, and the chances of its recurrence will go the opposite way.

It is quite clear that children are reinforced and punished in sex-stereotypical ways, although the nuances in these sex differences are sometimes described only by careful research. Moreover, we often forget that these powerful influences on behavior also exist for adult men and women, a point to which we will return later in this chapter. First, we examine the reward-punishment arrangements in childhood that are specific to males.

Boys Get Rewarded More Often Than Girls

In terms of basic *numbers* of rewards available, boys tend to have greater access.[14] This means that boys often learn that their behavior matters, and that they can influence their own lives. Clearly, this feedback has positive implications for achievement and sense of control. In fact, it is probably the most positive aspect of masculine gender training. As Ruth Hartley pointed out in her classic 1959 article on the socialization of the male child, "On the positive side, men mostly do what they want and are very important."[15]

Boys Get Punished More Often Than Girls

This fact has been demonstrated by a body of research that extends back several decades, and it has been confirmed by a recent large-scale study. Importantly, this is especially true for *physical* punishment.[16] In the 1950s and before, the conventional wisdom was, "Spare the rod and spoil the child." Psychologists know better now. Child development experts have discovered a number of negative effects of physical punishment. First, it leads to numerous highly unpleasant and destructive emotions, such as anger and a sense of violation. Second, it actually has the effect of *increasing* aggression in the child, perhaps as a result of these negative feelings, and teaching the child to associate violent behaviors with anger, frustration, or fear. Third, the child may develop chronically fearful or angry feelings toward the punisher. If this person is a parent, affiliation and closeness are inhibited. For these reasons, experts strongly recommend that physical punishment be used as a last resort and/or reserved for only those instances where the behavior poses an immediate danger, such as when the child runs into the street or reaches for a hot stove.[17]

We could speculate about the origins of sex differences in the amount and type of punishment. Clearly, there is a cultural sense that males are not hurt as much by physical pain or that this is the only way to control them. Boys also tend to have higher activity levels than girls (they are at least three times as likely to be hyperactive) and perhaps need to be controlled more often.

Fathers Do More Punishing Than Mothers

Despite the fact that fathers usually have considerably less contact with children than mothers, fathers more often find themselves in the parental punishing and controlling role.[18] As noted above, this arrangement may result in the association of negative feelings with the father. For boys, this may be especially troublesome, as fathers are probably the most important figures in their lives. To complicate matters, fathers tend to have fewer positive emotional interactions to offset the negative interactions, compared with mothers.

The parental practice of "wait until your father gets home" not only reinforces the negative outcomes we described, but it is also an almost completely ineffectual way of influencing the child's actions. For a punishment to be useful, it must follow the behavior immediately and be accompanied by the opportunity to learn the "correct" response. If a boy (or girl) waits several hours for the consequences of his behavior, he will not learn that he gets punished when he does something inappropriate, but rather that he gets punished when his father gets home. And, if the punishment is not understood, there is little opportunity for the child to correct his or her behavior. Many children learn to fear and resent their fathers for this reason alone.

What Do Boys Get Rewarded For?

Boys get rewarded for acting like little men. These rewards encourage such positive behaviors as problem solving as well as such relatively benign behaviors as achieving in athletics. They also encourage certain behaviors that are sometimes associated with more negative effects, such as rigidly controlling one's feelings and compulsively conforming one's behavior to external standards.

Males and females are also differentially rewarded for aggression. Developmental psychologist Eleanor Maccoby noted an interesting difference in the way boys' and girls' aggression is typically handled in schools. When girls show aggression, they are usually quietly reprimanded. However, boys' aggression often meets with loud protests from the teacher, and this response has the effect of stopping all of the action in the classroom and focusing everyone's attention on the acting-out boy.[19] For many children, negative attention is better than no attention at all. Many boys find out that aggression is a useful method for attaining social reward, a lesson that fewer girls learn.

WHAT IS THE SINGLE MOST POWERFUL GENDER SOCIALIZATION PROCESS FOR MALES?

Boys get punished more harshly and earlier in life for gender behaviors that are considered culturally inappropriate (i.e., "feminine" behaviors). Girls who are "tomboys" are socially accepted, at least until adolescence. Parents may even brag about their eight-year-old daughter who is active in her play and likes sports, but when is the last time you heard a parent speak glowingly about an eight-year-old boy who plays with dolls? A boy who acts in feminine ways is often called a "sissy"—perhaps the most shame-filled title possible. The tomboy and the sissy are equivalent in behavior, but there is a huge difference in the connotations that these labels carry.

A tendency to shame and punish boys for "feminine" activities begins as early as age three or four. This is, of course, a time when they have little understanding of why such gender distinctions are so important (in fact, we adults are not really so sure why). It is also a time when "feminine" behaviors seem quite necessary. He is too young to be independent. Most teachers are female; he must cooperate with them. He is too small and frail to be tough. He may be drawn to female classmates, but if he joins one of their play groups, he will almost surely be ostracized from his male peers. No such sanction seems to befall girls who join boys' groups.

The strong social disapproval of feminine behavior in males leads people (as pattern-seeking organisms) to define masculinity as *anti-femininity*, and so boys tend to learn what feminine behaviors are and then actively avoid them. This process leads to two profoundly negative outcomes. First, it prohibits males from engaging in a wide variety of behaviors that are satisfying, adaptive, and self-protective—for example, emotional self-disclosure, taking care of one's body, introspection, and finding pleasure in human relationships. Second, since males are socially viewed as more important and powerful than females, antifemininity encourages people, especially males, to devalue all that is feminine, including girls and women. Perhaps the most destructive component of hypermasculine socialization is that it strongly encourages men to view women with disrespect and even contempt.

Of the many research findings cited here, the discouragement of feminine behaviors in boys is one of the most robust. Therefore, if you find yourself asking, "Why don't males interact with females?" or "Why don't men express their 'feminine' sides?"; one answer is fairly straightforward—because it is often socially or even physically dangerous for them.

In conclusion, the systematic, gender-based rewards and punishments given to children result in intense pressure to act in accord with cultural conceptions of the masculine and the feminine. For most children, doing so involves going against naturally occurring, human tendencies. For instance, it is natural for a person to protect his or her body from harm. However, doing so (for instance, by refusing to play football) may result in social ostracization or some other form of punishment (or restricted access to rewards). Therefore, one may be influenced to ignore the naturally occurring tendency—in this case the instinct for self-preservation—and perform the prescribed but un-natural behavior. For many of the more negative masculine-defined behaviors, reward-punishment contingencies offer boys a choice be-tween being masculine and being human.

WHAT OTHER INFLUENCES
HAVE AN EFFECT ON BEHAVIOR?

One does not have to use reinforcement to establish behaviors. Children tend to simply imitate the behavior of those with whom they spend a lot of time, and those whom they perceive as being similar to themselves. In fact, most language acquisition is the result of imitation, not reward. Research evidence has determined that children are able to perceive sex differences very early in their lives, perhaps before age two.[20] Although there are many different ways in which people can be put into categories (e.g., by class, age, size, nationality, race, talent, attractiveness, personality characteristics, etc.), the category of male-female is probably the most basic of all, and this categorization is girded by the fact that we live in a very gender-stereotyped and gender-polarizing culture. (Note that people often use the term "opposite sex," forgetting that the sexes are in no way opposite. Rather, males and females are only slight variations within the same species with only one out of forty-six chromosomes that is different.) Therefore, children tend to learn very early in their lives that they are male or female, and they are more likely to imitate others of their same sex. They learn about categories and roles even before they learn about individuals, thus gaining a sense of *what* to be before they gain a sense of *whom* to be.

We can hardly overestimate the power of observation and imitation on a person's gendered behavior. Boys obviously imitate their fathers, male playmates, and other males with whom they come into contact, and much of this behavior is likely to be gender stereotypical. Research indicates that sons' levels of gender stereotyping closely re-semble those of their fathers.[21]

As behavioral scientists have discovered in the last thirty-five years, television and other media also have powerful influences on behavior. The average child will spend more hours in front of a television set before age six than he or she will spend in the classroom during an entire four years of college. If you take a close look at television and movies, you will find that gender stereotypes are very pervasive. Males are much more frequently presented as aggressive, task oriented, unfeeling, and achieving than females, who are more frequently presented as relationship oriented, emotional, and subservient.[22] Some of the most typical situation comedy plots involve stereotyped conflicts between men and women and depictions of men being incompetent in women's roles (child care, housework, relationships) and vice versa. Movies such as *Mr. Mom* and *Three Men and a Baby* derive much of their humor from men's incompetence in caring for children.

Television plays an especially pernicious role in encouraging violent behaviors among young males. Over 65 percent of major television characters are involved in violence each week, most of them males.[23] Through dramatic portrayals of violence, television and movie characters often teach that violence is an acceptable and effective way to solve problems and deal with conflict. Children with poor academic skills tend to behave aggressively, watch more television, and watch more violent programs, which tends to reinforce their aggression. Heightened aggression leads to more peer rejection, more isolation, and more television viewing. Thus, violent media are part of a vicious cycle of aggression for children, especially male children.

Media portrayals of gender also have important negative effects on the self-esteem of both males and females, according to researcher Mary Polce-Lynch and her colleagues.[24] Both male and female secondary school children report that comparing themselves with larger than life images makes them feel deficient, especially with regard to their bodies. It is impossible for most males to be great athletes or for most females to be thin and beautiful, and yet media often transmit the message that people who do not meet these ideals cannot be successful.

Of course, people are much more than passive recipients of reinforcement, punishment, and observation. Human beings think about, symbolize, and transform the information they receive, tending to place objects and events into categories, and making judgments based on these categories. Again, gender tends to top the list of categorizations of people, personality characteristics, and behaviors. A major idea placed into the mind of most boys very early in life is this: you should never have anything to do with females or anything labeled feminine. As we noted, the American concept of masculinity is really *antifemininity*, the avoidance of a great many behaviors, such as asking for help, expressing emotion, protecting oneself, being oriented toward relationships, and exploring one's inner life. Males are encouraged to take physical risks, be ruggedly independent, get the job done, never be satisfied, and live up to social standards of masculinity such as achievement in sports, sexual conquering, accumulation of wealth, and task focus.

HOW DO INDIVIDUAL MALES RESPOND TO MASCULINE SOCIALIZATION?

Social influences create pressures on men to behave in certain ways. Individual men react to these pressures differently. Some reject traditional masculinity and consciously attempt to counteract the strain caused by masculine demands. Others overemphasize male gender imperatives and act out the "macho" role. Most men struggle to find a comfortable compromise. Regardless of the strategy, the pressures to act according to gender expectations are always present. These demands, and the strain that goes with them, will not go away without social change.

How Is Masculine Socialization Perpetuated?

In a way, masculine gender socialization is somewhat like the hazing that takes place in fraternities, athletic teams, the military, and even in some aspects of the blue-collar or corporate working world. The "recruit" is made to suffer and must endure the pain silently to be accepted by the men in power. If he does so successfully, the recruit gains power through emotionally and behaviorally "buying into" the established system. He comes to value the system more highly (if he did not, he would have to think himself a fool for putting up with abuse), and thus he thinks of hazing as an appropriate and even "character-building" path to achievement. Just as fraternity members often romanticize their pledge period and military officers often idealize their boot camp experience, men frequently learn to distort the emotional and physical pain that accompanies harsh masculine socialization by rationalizing that it was beneficial to them. It is not unusual for an adult male survivor of physical abuse to say, "My daddy whipped me all the time, and it was the best thing he ever did for me. It taught me discipline and it taught me how to be a man." The acceptance and valuing of harsh masculine socialization leads men to pass this process down to their sons, their subordinates at work, and in other social settings.

It is important to keep in mind that the demand for antifemininity, which is so central to the masculine socialization process in childhood, continues to be enforced in the social worlds of adult men. Psychologist Robert Brannon asks what the typical reaction would be if one man said to another, "Mike, I've been so upset since we had that argument. I could hardly sleep last night. Are you *sure* you're really not mad at me?"[25] Men who act in feminine ways are ostracized, attacked, or neglected. Therefore, it is not only childhood socialization that keeps men within their narrow gender roles, it is also *ongoing* forces within the social environments of adult men. We are not suggesting that men learn to behave in the stereotypical way described by the above quote, but we do believe that men need to learn to break out of rigid gender boundaries to recover their full humanity.

WHAT ARE THE LINKS BETWEEN MASCULINE SOCIALIZATION AND GENDER IDENTITY?

Masculine socialization makes it very difficult to attain a positive sense of gender identity because of the following process:

1. Behaving in "masculine" ways is socially defined as *very* important.
2. However, boys do not really know how to be masculine. Many messages exist about not being feminine, but few clear and positive messages about being men. Fathers are frequently inaccessible (physically and/or emotionally) and boys are taught primarily by female teachers and child care providers. Boys often have to rely on older boys and media images of masculinity (which usually emphasize the stereotypical and often destructive aspects of masculinity) for information on how to behave in gendered ways.

3. Therefore, boys tend to feel anxious and inadequate about their masculinity.

4. But, males are supposed to be confident and independent, so they do not tend to ask for direction or information on gendered behavior. Imagine boys talking with each other and saying, "Do you know how to be a man? I don't. Maybe we should talk to our dads about it." These self-doubts are largely unconscious; boys rarely reflect on gender demands or even know that these demands exist. This lack of awareness, together with the masculine value placed on giving an appearance of self-assurance, keeps boys from learning that they have choices about how they behave with regard to gender.

5. Many boys learn to resolve this paradox by adhering to the stereotypical and therefore "safe" masculine gender identity in very rigid ways, i.e., by emphasizing the most obvious, exaggerated aspects of cultural masculinity: emotional constriction, physical risk, aggression, and the "macho" image.

Girls tend to form a sense of gender identity from frequent contact with adult women and from talking about femininity with other females. Note that this process is not without its pitfalls, but it does tend to create psychological issues that are different from those of males. In contrast, the way in which this mysterious masculinity is reinforced in boyhood establishes a *fantasized model* of masculinity. Having few concrete guidelines and real models of manliness, but knowing that this essence is vitally important, boys tend to extrapolate information from the extremes of masculine behavior that they observe in the culture. For example, when girls are asked what they want to be when they grow up, they tend to respond with relatively attainable (although also gender stereotypical) career options such as teacher or nurse. When boys are asked the same question, they tend to say that they want to be the president, an astronaut, a professional athlete, or some other option that is unrealistic for the vast majority of people.[26] Lacking real-life models, boys turn to fantasized models and base their expectations about life choices on these unrealistic icons of masculinity.

HOW DOES A FATHER'S INACCESSIBILITY INFLUENCE A BOY'S SOCIALIZATION?

Because fathers typically have less contact with their children than mothers, and because fathers' socialization does not prepare them for child care (few males spend significant amounts of time in their childhoods changing diapers, baby-sitting, playing with dolls, or thinking about themselves in relationship with others), they tend to rely more on gender stereotypes than on experience to guide them through parenting, and they tend to do so more with their sons than with their daughters. Perhaps because of the "hazing" process described above and their own gender anxiety, fathers tend to further reinforce and maintain traditional and narrow expressions of masculinity.

When a father is physically and/or emotionally absent from his son's life, the boy tends to turn to peers for guidance and information on behaving in masculine ways. The image of masculinity the boy forms is less human and realistic than it is for the son whose father nurtures and spends time with him. Therefore, a father who is distant encourages his son to adopt the fantasized model we discussed above. For instance, it is not unusual for a son to believe that his father has never been afraid nor sad in his life, since the boy has never seen any outward manifestations of these emotions in his father. The son does not have access to the father's inner experience, but at some level the son is aware of his own occasional fear and sadness. When he compares his inner experience of vulnerability with his father's outward appearance of invulnerability, he tends to feel inadequate, and he learns to erect defenses against this feeling. The effect is to make him less human and more stereotypically masculine.

HOW IS MASCULINE SOCIALIZATION LINKED TO MASCULINE DEPRESSION?

As we have stated earlier, the hallmark of depression is a pervasive sense of hopelessness and helplessness. The depressed person sees the self as having irreparable flaws in important life areas and living in a world that offers neither help, acceptance, nor the promise of a positive change in the future. Depression expert Martin Seligman describes the depressed person as one who interprets negative events in the follow-ing way: "It's me, it's forever, and it affects everything I do."[27] Depressed people see themselves as defective in some important and pervasive way. They sense that there is no solution to their problem and that they are doomed to a life of profoundly negative experiences.

Masculine socialization demands the impossible. If you are a so-called "real man," you are physical and athletic, attractive, wealthy, self-assured, competitive, courageous, hyperindependent, dominant, and risk taking. Feelings are supposed to be under control at all times. (During a nationally televised post-game interview, a basketball coach cried as he described how touched he was by his team's courage. A sportscaster then commented, "He needs to get control of those "aller-gies" [emotions].) Most men cannot live up to these expectations. Even if a man is very strong, fit, and a great athlete, he will probably sustain occasional injuries that will limit him temporarily or perma-nently, and he will certainly experience the deterioration of physical skills that comes with aging. Ordinary men are not especially attrac-tive, wealthy, nor athletic, especially considering the American de-mand to be "Number One"—a status that only a single person can occupy at any given time. Nobody can be absolutely independent or keep his feelings perpetually under control. The world is a place where people are interconnected, and we have strong feelings about things and people that are important to us; emotion is a fact of life. Therefore, a man who strives for these masculine ideals spends his time trying to fool the world and himself into thinking he is something that he is not. Inwardly, he knows at some level that he is sometimes fearful or unsure of himself, that he needs other people. As a result of hyper-masculine striving, he looks foolish, alienates other people, and be-comes disconnected from his emotional life. Men who accept and overvalue these masculine demands put themselves at considerable risk of feeling that they are never good enough, that they can't do anything about it, and that things will never change—hopelessness, helplessness, and worthlessness.

The negative definition of masculinity, i.e., masculine as "not femi-nine," produces an unresolvable deficit model of masculine value. Proving that you are manly requires you to prove that you are not feminine, and it is impossible to do so once and for all time. You may be able to act in a brave, unemotional, and dominant way today, but doing so does not mean that you won't be fearful, vulnerable, or weak tomorrow. Proving a negative is impossible. A man who accepts extreme notions of manliness must engage in a compulsive quest to demonstrate his masculine worth over and over again. Inevitably, some failure occurs, undermining his sense of self-worth and reminding him of his deficiencies. For some men, these seemingly continuous failures lead to depression.

Behaviorists such as B. F. Skinner have a slightly different way of looking at depression. Skinner viewed people as oriented toward attaining reward (or reinforcement) and avoiding punishment. In his opinion, depressed people are simply those who are unsuccessful at receiving much reinforcement and/or who are punished frequently.[28] One can probably find the highest concentrations of depressed people in prisons and other impoverished settings. The reason is obvious—there is little or nothing there that is pleasant (reinforcing) and the harsh environment offers nearly continuous punishment. Unfortunately, depressed men live in *psychological* prisons that have been constructed and maintained by families, the culture, and themselves.

We can conceptualize the masculinity-depression connection by taking a look at the expectations for what men are *not* supposed to be. If you are a so-called "real man," you are neither feminine, self-disclosing, fearful, relationship oriented, self-protective of body or feelings, nor cooperative. As it turns out, these behaviors are extremely important for attaining reward and avoiding punishment. For example, self-disclosure, the revealing of the self to trusted others, is crucial for reducing one's isolation and indispensable for the development of intimacy within a relationship. It is somewhat of an oversimplification to think of intimacy as merely repetitious reinforcement, but look at all the rewards that true intimacy produces: a person takes care of you emotionally, shares your joy and soothes your sorrow, provides companionship, and understands your struggles. People are not moved to take care of those who do not reveal themselves, nor to stick around if the other person is distant, uncaring, difficult to influence, and overly involved in things like sports and work. Like women, men crave intimacy—more than 90 percent marry at some time in their lives.[29] Masculine demands for withholding information about one's inner life, being hyperindependent, and denying one's emotional world directly impede the quest for a vast array of interpersonal rewards, thus leaving men to seek more transient and less satisfying rewards: alcohol, sexual conquest, work and sports achievement, and dominance.

In summary, masculine socialization powerfully affects the way a man thinks, experiences the self, constructs values, and interacts with others. While the masculine "system" offers many opportunities (money, achievement, discovery, perseverance in task completion, the admiration of others), the road to stereotypical manhood is fraught with emotional pitfalls that leave many men feeling inadequate, unfulfilled, isolated, self-alienated, and wounded. The acceptance of masculine social demands is an important ingredient in the recipe for masculine depression.

Chapter 4

The Masculine Dilemma: "Not Too Close, Not Too Far Away"

Masculine depression has numerous consequences for men's physical health, mental health, working life, and relationships. The focus of this chapter is the impact of masculine depression on the man's primary intimate relationship with his wife, girlfriend, or partner. It is in this relationship that men often play out the psychological dramas that are related to issues that we described in previous chapters—conflicts created in his family of origin and reactions to masculine social pressures. For a significant group of men, these issues create strongly mixed feelings about primary relationships—a basic and seeming unresolvable dilemma. In this chapter, we describe the emotional discomfort (often accompanied by extreme behaviors) associated with either being too intimate or too detached from one's partner. Fully understanding the consequences of masculine depression in intimate relationships sets the stage for the solutions that we will propose in the second half of this book.

At younger and more vulnerable stages of identity development, children spend the vast majority of their time with females, usually their mothers. One of the earliest psychological tasks for the child is to form an attachment to the primary caregiver. This basic attachment issue can create problems for a boy, who may develop a fear of psychological engulfment by his mother and her female identity.

All children, both male and female, experience this basic fear. Even infants will look away from an intense gaze when it becomes uncomfortable, intrusive, or overstimulating. In acquiring a sense of who they are and who they are not, engulfment (taking on or having someone else's identity take over, and becoming them instead of becoming oneself) represents a basic psychological danger. Boys

71

must somehow attach to their mothers and avoid engulfment at the same time. The tension of these opposing tasks in early relationships creates an emotional ambivalence that does not tend to be as pronounced for girls. Boys experience a conflict in which individual identity as male and being attached to a female can be at odds. This childhood conflict is often reactivated in adult relationships.

As we discussed in Chapter 2, boys often experience an inaccessible male model. It is in this void that boys must contend with a present and available female model. Girls' identity is based on their attachment with a female caregiver, but boys' identity is based on separation; they must establish themselves as not being female. In Chapter 3 we reviewed a socialization process that teaches boys that "how to be" (masculine, i.e., antifeminine) is more important than "who to be" (yourself as a unique individual). Unconscious conflicts arise for males, linking primary relationships involving females with an internal sense of anxiety and inadequacy (i.e., "Am I being 'not female' enough? Am I different enough from women?"). Boys' bodies grow and develop into men's, but these unconscious processes remain unchanged until they are noticed and worked through.

WHAT IS THE MASCULINE DILEMMA?

Boys learn they must stay "not too close, not too far away" from their mothers. The first part of the phrase, "not too close" means that a boy must defend himself psychologically against engulfment by his mother. When fathers provide primary nurturance and caregiving for boys, this fear does not tend to appear in such intensity. In that case, boys can be "daddy's little boy" and experience social approval for close and intimate attachment to another human being. But in the usual circumstances, boys' development does not include approval for attachment. Instead, a boy learns at an early age that it is dangerous to be a "mama's boy" and become overattached to a female (or, by extension, to characteristics within himself that the culture labels as "feminine").

The opposite of engulfment is abandonment. Children greatly fear being left alone. They understand at a deep level that they are unable to provide for themselves emotionally and physically. Physical abandonment represents physical starvation and death. Emotional abandonment represents the symbolic parallel of emotional starvation. The second part of the phrase "not too far away" is a reminder to guard against the fear of abandonment and possible psychological death.

The dilemma "not too close, and not too far away" defines a traditional masculine theme in relationships with intimate partners. It is unconscious, and therefore it remains unchanged until it is noticed and resolved in adult relationships. The unconscious part of the mind does not recognize time, places, and individuals. It is activated by emotional associations. If there is a significant conflict in a primary and dependent relationship with a woman, the unconscious mind later generates the fear embedded in that conflict when an emotional association is made. Thus, the early childhood masculine dilemma is recapitulated in adult intimate relationships with women.

As with many psychological themes, that which was adaptive in childhood can be limiting and destructive in adulthood. The masculine dilemma artificially controls intimacy in a marriage, frustrating both the man and the woman. Neither partner can experience a satisfying relationship under this circumstance. She cannot get close to him, and he cannot overcome his unconscious and automatic fear when he senses her emotional closeness.

The use of traditional masculinity in defense of a tenuous gender identity begins in the family of origin, continues through the socialization process, and manifests itself again in adult relationships. One possible solution in early childhood lies in providing more frequent and meaningful contact between boys and their fathers. In fact, cultures in which men participate actively in child care show evidence of fewer displays of masculine dominance, fewer expectations of women's deference to men, and less of an ideology of female inferiority.[1] In cultures where fathers and sons tend to have a low degree of contact (such as mainstream United States culture), boys and men rely on unnatural and unhealthy beliefs about females to manage the rigors of masculine development. Healthy attachment to fathers has positive benefits in adult heterosexual relationships.

WHAT DOES THE MASCULINE DILEMMA LOOK LIKE?

It looks like this: a man who has never missed a day of work in his life cannot function on the job when he fears that his wife has interests in another man. Even though a man seeks out and marries a woman he dearly loves, in the middle of a conflict he hits her!? A strong, successful man contemplates suicide when his wife leaves him!? How could these things happen? We believe that behaviors like these are expressions of a seemingly irreconcilable dilemma, the masculine dilemma, in which men desperately attempt to stay "not too close and not too far away." The only means available to negotiate this dilemma are a range of destructive behaviors. Masculine depression affects men's relationships in many ways, and the masculine dilemma is the major manifestation of masculine depression within the context of a primary heterosexual relationship. By remaining "not too close, not too far away," men dissociate from their feelings about dependency and attachment and act in ways that are destructive to intimate relationships. When men experience frustration, loneliness, or failure (experiences not uncommon in relationships), masculine depression predisposes men to expressions of the type that we have described.

As boys grow to become men, the masculine dilemma creates more relationship difficulties, which in turn deepen masculine depression. Men continually face the dilemma of wanting and needing relationships, yet they experience confusion, hurt, misunderstandings, and failure in these relationships. When a depressed man engages in a relationship, his actions become a distortion of his inner experiences. His behavior ("the outside") doesn't match his feelings ("the inside"). He looks angry when he is fearful. He looks quiet and detached when he most needs to talk. Because of the limitations of traditional masculinity, vulnerable feelings are converted to aggressive and aloof behaviors in the context of complex intimate relationships. Traditional masculinity provides temporary safety from threats during the socialization process. Sustaining intimate adult relationships require other, more long-term types of skills.

HOW DOES DISSOCIATION FROM FEELINGS CONTRIBUTE TO THE MASCULINE DILEMMA?

How many times have you spoken with a man or boy who couldn't quite find the right word to describe how he felt? More than likely, you were clued in by his behavior that he was "feeling" something painful.

Happy people behave differently from sad, angry, or frightened people. If a male cannot express his hurt, sadness, loneliness, emptiness, or fear in a direct way, his feelings will find another form of expression. It is human nature that feelings which are not felt or understood at the basic level (i.e., "I'm afraid") are acted out in behaviors. To use a simple example, it is natural to be nervous or afraid about going on a date. A healthy/normal experience would be to talk with a friend about how frightened you feel. But most men or boys may not even be aware of their anxiety because their feelings have been numbed out for many years. Or they may feel intimidated into not expressing these feelings. So instead, they may drink to "calm their nerves." The man may not even notice his anxiety until he does something foolish like trip and fall, or until he notices that his hand is shaking. Perhaps the saddest part of all is that men don't get what they need most in those frightening moments (comfort and reassurance) because they have been conditioned not to "feel" or not to express feelings. They have learned their lesson too well.

To be separated from one's emotions is to be dissociated from feelings. As a result, these feelings cannot be expressed in direct and healthy ways. Instead, they find expression in behaviors or in physical ills. Men who do not feel or express emotions are much more likely than other men to "explode" and react with physical or psychological violence. The underlying feeling may be fear, vulnerability, despair, self-doubt, etc. But when feelings remain dissociated the resulting behavior can be irrational and dangerous. Men often hurt those whom they love most—their partners and their children. In those moments of rage, men cannot "feel" their vulnerability. Because they cannot access their own pain, they cannot empathize with the pain that they cause to others. They may feel extremely remorseful after they have caused the damage, but they cannot feel anything but anger in the moment when they most need to experience vulnerable feelings and control their anger.

HOW DO MEN AND WOMEN TEND TO DIFFER IN A RELATIONSHIP?

Male development predisposes men to separate and to be autonomous. Self-sufficiency is of primary importance to most men's self-concepts. Female social development is more likely to lead to a deeper appreciation of being a part of relationships with others, with all of the difficulties that these relationships bring. As a result, women tend to "join" better than men. Thus, men are presented with more difficulties than women in negotiating all kinds of relationships, especially the marital one. Because an intimate relationship requires more joining than separating, a marriage is weakened, sometimes to the point of dissolution, if it involves more separating than joining. The male's learned style of autonomy and separateness contributes more to dissolving than to maintaining marriages.

While both men and women face ambivalence in intimate relationships, women are more likely to be taught how to prepare for these mixed feelings and how to deal with them. Men, on the other hand, often find themselves unprepared for relationship problems and, in fact, they are socialized to avoid mixed feelings. Many men do not fully understand that relationships intrinsically involve ambivalence and conflict. Therefore, they feel threatened by relationship difficulties and react with counterproductive masculine behaviors (such as aggression or detachment) that allow them to feel more psychologically protected in the moment.

A healthy intimate relationship is very helpful (some would argue essential) to psychological survival. However, the skills and behaviors necessary to establish and maintain an intimate relationship are completely incompatible with the defensive strategy of traditional masculinity. True intimacy requires one to trust, reveal emotions, be dependent on occasion, share power, and cooperate. Traditional masculinity requires a person to be cautious, guarded, in control, independent, overpowering, and dominant. It is impossible to be "macho" and intimate at the same time.

How Does the Masculine Dilemma Become Activated in a Relationship?

All relationships involve occasional conflict. For many men, there seems to be no "right way" (i.e., no perfectly reliable formula) to successfully negotiate a conflict with a woman. If he "gives in," he feels like he loses; if he fights the way he is socialized to fight, i.e., to win, he still feels like he loses. Giving in represents engulfment; "winning" distances him from her and represents abandonment. There are no other men to help guide him—he's on his own, armed with the behaviors associated with the masculine defense that he has had to learn so well. Marriages and intimate relationships require an entirely different set of coping strategies, yet to ask for them, he would first have to violate the rules he has come to live by. Because of these complexities, marriages can expose the behavioral manifestations of men's depression by setting off the range of behaviors and physical problems that we have previously described.

Masculine depression is not only triggered in marriages. Men also become depressed by work, the stress of living, and other conflicts or failures. However, masculine depression triggered by these other sources can then cause marital conflict when these stresses are acted out at home. When a man behaves in abrupt, rude, or insensitive ways (e.g., because he is hurt or was passed over for a promotion), it is difficult to treat these behaviors as communications about inner feelings of sadness. They do not look or feel like depression to the other person.

HOW DOES THE MASCULINE DILEMMA AFFECT INTIMACY?

Men experience confusion about the meaning and experience of intimacy. Interpersonal intimacy involves dependence *and* independence. Most men think of dependence as an unmasculine, and therefore, a bad thing, as it implies a loss of control over a situation. In place of healthy interdependence between partners, traditional masculinity introduces the need to defend against attack and guard against losing. But relationships rely partly on some degree of healthy dependence, which is closely linked to trust between partners. In a healthy relationship, one partner can depend on the other to be faithful and supportive. Traditional masculinity labels dependence as a form of femininity, something for men to avoid. In an intimate heterosexual relationship, a man fears that dependence means that he is being "whipped" by his wife. If she makes her own independent decisions in the family, it may feel to him like something is terribly wrong.

These kinds of cultural images influence men and women to see each other as adversaries, yet true intimacy requires cooperation.

When people ask, "Who wears the pants in the family?" or "Who has the upper hand in the relationship?" there is an implication that there must be dominance and power struggle in male/female relationships. Many relationships have this character, but they do not have to. In fact, research indicates that relationships which stand the test of time are based on communality and shared goals rather than bargaining and exchange.[2]

Every relationship includes a power element. In a healthy relationship, partners share power and depend on each other. In an unhealthy relationship, people compete for power and strive to keep the other person's influence to a minimum. A traditional man may think of his relationship with his business partner as one of cooperation, trust, and interdependence. Success in business is partly the product of dependence and trust. But, because of the expectation of men's dominance of women and some of the other dynamics we have discussed throughout this book, the same man may believe that his relationship with his wife has to be one of mistrust, posturing, and overpowering. He does whatever he can to avoid any dependence on her.

It is impossible to have a healthy relationship without some degree of dependence, and, in order to maintain an image of masculine control, men want to keep it a secret that they are dependent on their wives in any way. Sometimes a man is so successful at doing this that it is a secret even from himself, only to be revealed when she leaves him or defies the authority that he believes to be his.

Like successful business partners, successful couples have shared goals which partners work together to achieve. Doing so requires each partner to allow himself/herself to be influenced by the other— a kind of dependence that does not mesh well with traditional masculine styles of competition and dominance. Most men must learn a different style of relating in order to participate in a successful intimate relationship

Men who feel insecure about their dependence sometimes disguise it behind behaviors that we have come to label as *counterdependent* or *oppositional*. The difference between true independence and counterdependence is as follows. Independence means acting in a certain way because of an important goal or conviction, even though doing so means that one chooses to go against another's wishes on occasion. Sometimes, it means that one chooses to depend on someone else because of a shared commitment to the relationship. Counterdependence means acting in a certain way to demonstrate or prove the absence of any dependence—to go against the other person in order to maintain an appearance of power. Independent behaviors say, "I make my own decisions so that I can do what is important, even when it goes against the grain." Counterdependent behaviors say, "You're not going to tell *me* what to do; I'll do whatever I want, and whatever I choose to do cannot have anything to do with trusting or depending on you." Figure 4.1 illustrates the three psychological stances of dependence, independence, and counterdependence.

Counterdependence is often disguised as independence, and sometimes it is difficult to tell one from the other. The following example will serve as an illustration of the difference: A couple gets into conflict over the husband's too-frequent business trips. The wife, feeling abandoned by her husband, says, "Don't go to Philadelphia this week; stay home and we'll do something together."

The independent man's psychological reaction might look something like this: " I know she wants me to stay. I've always taken the trip. I could stay because it's important to her, or go on the trip because it's important to my job. I can choose freely." If he chooses to go on the trip, he might say something such as, "I'm sorry to leave you alone again, but this trip is very important. Let's find a time when I return to do something special together, and maybe there's a way to negotiate with my boss so my trips are not so frequent." Although there is conflict and disagreement, his response acknowledges her feelings and suggests a solution that might be comfortable for both partners.

In contrast, a counterdependent psychological stance is, "She can't tell me what to do. If I cooperate with her or it will mean that she'll overpower me. Just to prove that she can't control me, I'll go on the trip whether I want to or not." He might respond to her as follows: "Hey, you can't tell me what to do. It's *my* work and I'm going to go on the trip no matter what you say. Why don't you just drop what *you're* doing and come along on the trip? That's what you'd do if you really wanted to support me."

FIGURE 4.1. The Three Psychological Stances of Dependence,
Independence, and Counterdependence

Fear of abandonment
("I'm lost without you")

↗

DEPENDENCE

↘

Dependent behavior
(clinging, begging, blind obedience)

Confident and self-sufficient
("I like being with you, but I can also be
on my own")

↗

INDEPENDENCE

↘

Independent behavior
(mature and respectful interactions)

Fear of engulfment
(I cannot allow you to get close to me)

↗

COUNTERDEPENDENCE

↘

Counterdependent behavior
(being oppositional, engaging in power
struggles)

Note that the behavior may be the same in both instances—he goes on the business trip. In the independent scenario, he shows a desire and a willingness to respect his wife's feelings and negotiate a change. In the counterdependent scenario, he postures for the power position and further damages the relationship. When partners lose their trust in each other and become adversarial, they engage in repeated power struggles. If one partner uses counterdependent power tactics too often, the other partner's only recourse is to use the same tactics. Interdependence means mutual and uncoerced choices, and people must be able to choose to put the partner first sometimes in order to have a cooperative and healthy relationship. If one cannot do so, then one will turn to coercive measures: bullying, abandonment, and passive aggression. The masculine dilemma encourages men to use these tactics to maintain the tenuous position of "not too close, not too far away." When men use these tactics habitually, their wives must also adopt them to have some influence in the relationship.

Counterdependence is normal in two developmental stages: early childhood and early adolescence, when identity issues are highlighted in primitive ways. The parents of two-year-olds talk about the "terrible twos" when children are oppositional, seemingly doing things just to anger their parents and deciding that "no" is their favorite word. Parents of fourteen-year-olds have similar complaints about their children—"he/she seems to fight me just for the sake of fighting." Both stages involve highly provocative behavior that makes the parent/child relationship very difficult. In both cases, parents often resort to coercive measures when they feel helpless to do anything else. Parents of two-year-olds may physically prevent them from doing what they want to do. Parents of fourteen-year-olds often "lay down the law" and appeal to their position of authority. ("As long as you're under my roof, you'll do what I say.")

Children at these ages behave in this way because they are trying to establish a sense of their own identity, and oppositionalism is a primitive way to begin to do so. As an old psychoanalytic saying goes, "The statement of what one *is* begins with a statement of what one *is not.*" When children work through the identity issue to a degree of resolution, they no longer need to use oppositional behavior. Two-year-olds become more cooperative as they progress through childhood. Later in life, when adult identity issues begin to surface, they again have a tendency to become oppositional as young adolescents, but most grow out of it again as they mature and gain self-confidence.

We have already discussed how a depressed man has a tenuous sense of gender identity, even when other aspects of his identity are quite solid. We have also discussed the negative definition of masculinity as being the "not feminine." These two difficulties are part of the recipe for counterdependence. When the masculine dilemma is highlighted in a relationship, the depressed man responds like a two- or a fourteen-year-old, as if to say, "I don't know who I *am* (as a man), but I am *not* you (connected and cooperative). So I can't cooperate or give you what you want because you might engulf me and I might lose my identity."

To show how far counterdependence can go, we will replay the earlier conflict and take it a little bit further:

> **She:** "Don't go to Philadelphia this week; stay home and we'll do something together."
>
> **He:** "Hey, it's *my* work and I'm going to go on the trip no matter what you say. Why don't you just drop what *you're* doing and come along on the trip? That's what you'd do if you really wanted to support me."
>
> **She:** "Okay, if that's the way you want it, that's what I'll do!"
>
> **He:** "Come on, you know that won't work! I'll be busy all the time and you'll be even madder than you are now."

His last statement exposes his counterdependence—he has rejected *his own suggestion!* The fact that he is doing so is a strong indication that he never expected her to take him up on it; he only suggested it in order to maintain his control over the situation.

While it appears to be independent, counterdependent behavior is really a disguised dependence. His behavior depends on hers, but instead of going *along with* anything she says (which would be dependent), he goes *against* anything she says. This strategy allows him to feel masculine and in control, but it comes at a high price, and, interestingly, he is not in control at all.

So, as men confuse independence with counterdependence, men establish a way of being in a relationship that is fundamentally detrimental to that relationship. Men function in a counterdependent manner thinking that they are independent. They are in fact destroying a relationship that requires both dependence and independence, not counterdependence.

We can see in counterdependence some of the same themes that we have developed elsewhere in this book—behaviors that are complete distortions, sometimes even opposites, of underlying feelings. Just as counterdependence is disguised dependence, bravado is disguised fear, narcissism is disguised self-doubt, and masculine depression is disguised depression. These classic, destructive masculine behaviors hide the pain behind the mask, making the treatment of the pain very difficult, and causing relationship problems at every turn.

Masculine depression presents itself in intimate relationships as the masculine dilemma. "Not too close, not too far away" defines and limits men's behavior in adult relationships. The masculine dilemma summarizes the effects of traditional masculinity on men's lives and those around them. "Not too close, not too far away" started with an emotionally isolated father in the boy's family. Because the conflicts from this early experience remain unconscious and unresolved, men grow into the same patterns as their fathers.

Summary of Part I

We have presented a model for understanding male development with the purpose of making sense out of behavior that does not make sense. By looking at family development through a gender lens we see how males face subtle but defining differences in early relationships. We see how masculine identity is initially based on an *oppositional* stance—being "not mother," rather than an *affiliative* stance—being "like father." The oppositional stance in relation to females is often entrenched in the masculine socialization process. Because of the harsh punishment boys receive for gender role violations, boys learn to scorn and devalue femininity. The purpose of this devaluation is to keep men safely hidden behind a mask of masculinity, feeling superior to women and safe from the attacks of other men.

Males develop with both an uncertainty about their identities and a fear of female identity. Because masculinity is defined in the negative, men cannot once and for all achieve an unthreatened sense of being masculine, and traditional masculinity becomes an ongoing process of psychologically defending oneself from the unconscious but perceived threat of femininity. In families, males defend against engulfment and abandonment without a clear model of how to do so successfully. When boys look for a male model, too often they see a father isolated from emotional connections and behaving in traditionally masculine ways. Boys both model this form of masculinity and feel inadequate in doing so. Their early relationships with their mothers can generate fears of intimacy. These forces on the development of boys remain unspoken, unconscious, and unresolved. Later, intimate relationships and family life reactivate these conflicts in adulthood.

By the time they become adults, males have learned through the socialization process how to appear masculine. They have learned that adhering to gender stereotypes is very important, as they have been punished harshly and frequently for gender role violations, beginning at a very early age. Often, they do not really learn about how to be men from healthy sources. Traditional masculinity is a defense that offers temporary safety from social shame and punishment for not behaving in masculine ways.

Conflicted boys become depressed men, with unresolved and unconscious conflicts about masculine identity and fears of revealing their inner selves to friends, intimate partners, or even to themselves. In adult relationships men learn to control intimacy by remaining "not too close, not too far away." As an extension of traditional masculinity, "not too close, not too far away" creates apparent safety in a relationship by limiting full emotional expression, and it has the unfortunate effect of limiting intimacy in a relationship.

PART II:
REMEDIES

Introduction to Part II

We began this book by stating that an accurate conceptualization of a problem is a necessary precondition to solving that problem. Part I is our proposed conceptualization. We have shown that masculine depression can be disguised by a variety of destructive and inappropriate behaviors, and that therefore it is often unrecognized, undiagnosed, untreated, and misunderstood. We have sought to present a model of masculine depression that neither victimizes nor pathologizes men, but instead provides an understanding from which men can begin to undertake the process of healthy change. An accurate understanding of the pain behind the mask can lead to effective interventions that address not only the symptoms of masculine depression, but also the underlying problems that cause those symptoms.

Theory drives intervention, and the remedies that we will offer in Part II follow in a logical progression from the model we presented in Part I. We believe that the origins and consequences of masculine depression are intertwined with the relationships in an adult man's life, especially with his intimate partner. In the following chapters, we offer relationship interventions based on the central features of masculine depression: dissociated feelings and destructive behaviors.

In Chapter 5, we address the first impaired relationship in the depressed man's life, his relationship to his inner self. We start here because, while most people may not think in terms of having a relationship with oneself, this aspect of experience sets the tone for all other relationships. People who think of themselves as competent or incompetent, lovable or unlovable, etc., have usually developed these opinions of the self in relationship with important people in their lives, and they may then treat themselves and others in ways that maintain the original messages. Most men are encouraged to present themselves to others as autonomous, masterful, and competent. Underneath this presentation, they may or may not feel this way. The relationship to self may be characterized by comfort, peace, and trust in the self, or by doubt, fear and other negative evaluations.

A man's ability to change his behavior and accept new responsibilities hinges on his relationship with himself. If that relationship is based on fear, doubt, and anxiety, he may react to the need to change with defensiveness and opposition. Accepting the need to change would require him to acknowledge his faults, and masculine defenses work directly against his doing so. When a man comes to terms with himself in a way that allows him to deal with his pain, he can accept responsibility for his behavior and change in healthy ways.

Chapter 6 addresses a man's relationships with other men. Our premise is that a vitally important component of traditional masculinity is an unspoken relationship with other men. You may recall that, in Chapter 3, we reviewed the extent to which males are punished for gender role violations. The harshest of this punishment comes from other males, and it can have a lasting effect on a man's behavior and sense of self. Healthy masculinity means having one's value as a man affirmed by other men as well as by the self. When men stop attacking and threatening one another, they can explore their masculinity without fear, anxiety, and suspicion.

Perhaps the most profound impaired relationship in the depressed man's life is with his emotionally unavailable father who fails to nurture healthy male attachments. As we also discussed in Chapter 3, the problematic paternal relationship leads to defensive postures in relationship to other males. Healing the wounds from this early relationship not only changes the way that one experiences being a man, it also changes the ways in which men relate to their partners. An important part of this healing can take place in the company of men.

From there, we turn our attention to men's relationships with women. All too often, women are the only source of men's comfort, support, healing, and nurturing. Men cannot be comforted and healed while simultaneously being aloof and hyperindependent. As we examined in Chapter 4, no relationship can be satisfying until a man addresses and resolves the masculine dilemma of "not too close, not too far away." In Chapter 7, we offer specific techniques to help men to safely address their fears and develop meaningful relationship skills within the context of their primary intimate relationships.

We then return to families. We presented a view of family relationships that initiate gender-specific development in Chapter 2. In Chapter 8, we show that child rearing provides an opportunity for men to end the destructive intergenerational cycle of masculine depression. When boys can comfortably attach to their fathers, masculine development can be positively defined—"I am masculine by being like Dad" instead of negative—"I am masculine by being not like Mom." The negative definition of identity is defensive; the positive is affirming.

Social norms permit men to express only one emotion: anger. As we have noted throughout this book, traditionally masculine men tend to convert most other emotions into angry feelings. In Chapter 9, we address the most destructive expression of men's anger: violent behavior, including that which is directed toward loved ones. All men have a responsibility, not only to avoid violence at all costs, but also to use their influence to persuade other men to do so. New insights into masculinity present new challenges for men of conscience, and Chapter 9 includes suggestions for how men can become involved in anti-violence efforts in their neighborhoods, communities, and the culture at large.

Our final chapter addresses a major, yet frequently overlooked outcome of masculine depression. Men die an average of seven years younger than women, have higher death rates for all fifteen leading causes of death, and engage in high-risk behaviors affecting their health.[1] These behaviors include failing to use health care services, engaging in activities with potential for physical injuries, not eating a healthy diet, and overindulging in drinking, sexual activities, and dangerous sports. Traditional masculinity is as destructive to men as it is to those in relationships with men. Chapter 10 is directed toward helping men overcome the traditional masculine barriers to caring for their physical health.

Part II is dedicated to providing a model for healthy masculinity. Utilizing the insights from the model that we presented in the first four chapters, we define relationships as the context for developing healthy relationships with self, other men, intimate partners, families, and communities.

Chapter 5

Empathy for Self
and Responsibility for Change

Jack thought that he was a failure. He felt guilty for the way he had avoided his wife over many years. He had overinvested himself in his work, left her alone on weekends and holidays, and rarely talked to her about her interests or his. She felt lonely and neglected, and she had become increasingly depressed in recent months. The more pain he saw in her eyes, the more shame he felt. He believed that her pain was his fault. However, he could not talk with his wife about it when he felt this bad. It was as if the manner in which Jack realized the problem made the solution more difficult. He was immobilized by shame. His guilt about the pain he had brought his wife caused him to avoid her even more. He could not face himself, thinking that he was the kind of man who could cause such pain.

In a therapy session with Jack, I reviewed family development and socialization processes that lead to the "not too close, not too far away" dilemma for men. He saw how these themes fit for him, but he continued to see his behavior in the marriage as evidence of his being a failure and thus a "bad" man. I remarked to him, "You know, Jack, it's not your fault. You didn't design the family structure or socialization process that brought you here. You did not cause this pain in your family because you knew you had other choices. You didn't know how to form a relationship in any other way. However, it is your responsibility to do something about the problem."

After a moment, Jack's body seemed to change, as if a weight had been lifted from his shoulders. He said that it helped to understand, "I didn't want this to happen. I am not a bad person because I wasn't able to 'do it correctly' but now I have the responsibility of changing myself to be a better husband for my wife." Jack was then able to move into an earnest discussion of the behaviors and habits that maintained the distance between them and how he could and would change each of them. He understood himself. His wife's pain was not evidence of his malicious intentions, but a result of his best attempt at resolving the masculine dilemma. He knew that he could *do* better because he *wanted* to do better. He was committed to putting in the necessary time and effort required to do so.

Jack gave himself a break, and doing so helped him to take responsibility for changing his behavior. He could see that he had been subjected to inhumane treatment in his family of origin and that he had responded by behaving in inhuman ways with his wife. He began to have empathy for himself. Once Jack understood his own pain, he also understood that he did not want to be an avoiding and neglectful husband. His accurate empathy for his own feeling led Jack to embrace responsibility for changing the way he identified and communicated his feelings to his wife. Although Jack's initial view of the problem helped him to have empathy for his wife's feelings, it did not help him to change his behavior. It was empathy for himself that got him "unstuck."

When Jack stepped outside of himself and saw himself as a person, he could see with compassion and empathy the "masculinizing" processes that had both hurt and limited him. He could see that many of these developmental influences were destructive for him and had caused him an emotional pain of which he was only vaguely aware. His unrecognized emotional pain kept him hidden from his wife and from himself. Once he understood this pain, he not only could take responsibility for changing his behavior, he was eager to do so. He wanted to change, and the first change had to be in relation to himself. He needed to see himself as someone who is worthy of love and wanting to love. He needed to understand that he was entitled to both have his feelings and to share them with his wife. Jack could be more emotionally intimate with his wife when he understood his feeling and was not filled with shame and the fear of being a failure.

*   *   *

We start with the concept of *empathy* because it is one of the major antidotes to masculine depression. Traditional masculinity tells men that to fail is to *be* a failure, to feel unsure is to *be* weak, to admit a shortcoming is to *be* a loser. These distorted ways of thinking prevent healthy relationships and effective change. To fail, feel unsure, or admit a shortcoming is to be a less-than-perfect human being. Traditional masculinity demands perfection but breeds masculine depression. When men try hard to grow and develop, they are worthy of support and encouragement. Harsh, unforgiving interpretations of their behavior obstruct healthy relationships because they limit men to defensive or overcompensating positions in relation to another person and even to themselves. When men defend and hide fears of inadequacies instead of revealing feelings, they are more likely to view themselves negatively.

The first challenge that men must face in the process of change is in relationship to themselves. If they are to break the destructive patterns of masculine depression, the place to start is with empathy for themselves. Inhumane treatment needs to be recognized before inhuman behavior can fully change. Men need to:

1. recognize their own feelings, i.e., understand their destructive behavior as a distorted expression of their desire to love and connect, and as a need to protect themselves,
2. recognize the negative effects of male development, i.e., understand their behavior as a reflection of their learning, not as a reflection of what they wanted to learn, and
3. learn ways to express themselves that do not maintain the destructive pattern of emotional dissociation that is central to traditional masculinity, i.e., learning to name, experience, and share feelings.

In this chapter, we will describe an initial process of learning about dissociated feelings and discuss why it is important to start with feelings instead of thoughts or behaviors. We will present ways in which men can learn to relate to themselves through the process of developing empathy for themselves and for others.

We begin our remedies for masculine depression with one of its two defining characteristics—dissociated feelings. We believe that destructive behaviors do not fully change until the man learns how to recognize and express his feelings in healthier ways.

WHAT DO "DISSOCIATED FEELINGS" FEEL LIKE?

By definition, dissociated feelings are not experienced consciously or expressed directly. Instead they are experienced unconsciously and expressed indirectly through behaviors that act out the emotion and/or as physical symptoms. As we have stated, when men feel anger, sadness, confusion, or hurt, they may yell at their wives, develop back problems, go on a drinking binge, or find themselves unable to turn off their minds and go to sleep. It is often difficult for people to believe that a man may be so cut off from his emotional life that he does not even know that he feels sad. These outward behaviors and symptoms—"masks"—distract everyone (often including the man himself) from seeing what caused the pain in the first place. Instead of seeing a person who hurts emotionally, others see a grouch, a workaholic, or a person with evil intent. The dissociative process distorts the real expression and communication of feelings.

Feelings never lie, and they never lie still. Even in dissociated form, they find expression in one form or another. A man may not notice his anger, the rise in his blood pressure, or his sudden annoyance at a son's loud playing. Nevertheless, the feeling was expressed, even though it slipped by his conscious awareness, thus becoming disconnected or dissociated from his experience.

We see how dissociated feelings are expressed in this interaction with a male college student during a first session at a typical university counseling center.

Counselor: What brings you to the center?

Client: Well, I've been having some problems lately with concentrating in my classes, motivation, studying—stuff like that. I've been having some trouble getting to sleep at night. When I finally do fall asleep, it's four in the morning, so then I end up sleeping past noon, which makes me miss most of my classes.

Counselor: And how long have you been having these problems?

Client: I'd say about four or five weeks.

Counselor: Anything that happened around the time you started having these difficulties?

Client: Well, you know, it was about midterm time and so the school pressure started building up, and I was falling behind, and also this girl broke up with me. . .

Counselor: Really? And how did you feel about that?

Client: Well, I feel she shouldn't have done it. . .

This particular scene takes place time and time again in college counseling centers. Note that when the counselor asks about *feelings*, the client gives him *thoughts*. In the masculine world, feelings are something one does not pay attention to. This client was probably dissuaded from emotional expression and experience from an early age. His male friends probably continue this discouragement of emotional expression in their interactions with him. Yet it is his feelings, not his thoughts, that are troubling him.

At the end of this first counseling interview, it is typical for the therapist to ask, "Do you have a sense of what, specifically, you would like me to help you with to help you handle this problem?" In response to this question, a male client commonly says, "I want you to help me learn how to *not think about* the breakup." In other words, he is asking the counselor to help him polish the masculine defenses that do not seem to be working at the moment, i.e., to help him get better at dissociating from his feelings. If he were able to name and express his feelings and have empathy for himself instead of avoiding himself, he would be better able to grieve the loss of the relationship in a healthy and adaptive way.

The masculine family and socialization process we have described earlier make it difficult for men to deal with grief or any other vulnerable emotions. Look at the differences in the reactions of typical male and female peer groups when a person tells friends that he or she has been "dumped?" In a group of women, the usual response is support and the encouragement of emotional expression. Women are likely to say, "Tell me all about it," and "Go ahead and cry; you need to." They may hug and hold their grieving friend.

Male peer groups are more likely to say, "Let's go have a beer," or "We've got to find you another woman." Both of these responses discourage the man's expression of emotion. The first defines a goal of dulling one's feelings with a drug in order to distract him (since vulnerable feelings are regarded as nuisances or signs of weakness). The second response redefines emotional pain as a task, one of replacing the lost "object" (as if women were interchangeable!). The prevalent masculine value is the dominance of the heart by the head, and when masculine approaches to feelings do not provide relief, men may react by seeing themselves as failures. They may think, "If that's how men solve problems, why do I still feel so bad—maybe it's because there is something wrong with me. I can't let anyone know how I really feel or they will also see it."

HOW DO FEELINGS FIND EXPRESSION?

Feelings have only three avenues of expression. They can be expressed:

1. Consciously, usually through the verbal disclosure of feelings to a trusting confidant
2. Unconsciously through somatic complaints such as weight problems, high blood pressure, skin disorders, etc.
3. Unconsciously through disturbed behavior such as violence, yelling, avoidance, pouting, etc. ("acting out")

Someone who has been out of touch with his feelings for a significant period of time will most likely have a history of physical problems and/or behaviors that create problems for himself and those around him. His body, life style, and behavior will be littered with symptoms. When a man is asked how he is *feeling*, a disconnected man will tell you only what he is *thinking* because many men have neither the awareness nor the vocabulary to answer the question. (Although this problem is more likely to occur in men, it can also happen to women, as mainstream United States culture values rational and logical thinking over emotional awareness.)

As a lighthearted look at this issue, we present the top five responses most often given by men to the question, "How do you feel?"

5. "About what?"
4. "With my hands."
3. "Huh?"
2. "I think that . . ."

And the number one answer:

1. "I don't know. Honey, how do I feel?"

HOW DO YOU BEGIN TO FEEL FEELINGS?

Language is an important tool for symbolizing one's experience, and it is very useful in men's quest to recover their emotional lives. The first step in feeling feelings is to recognize a response and name it. Many men initially experience these responses in symptomatic form. The language of symptoms, i.e., disturbed behavior or health/life style impairments, does not look like the original feeling. Men need a way to translate symptoms back into original feelings.

Feelings do not come with names or flashing neon signs. There is no sudden announcement, "You are now feeling ashamed." In the beginning of this process, it is helpful to use a brief listing of feelings and "try each one on" to see which one or ones fit for a certain situation. An easy feelings word list is:

MAD

SAD

GLAD

AFRAID

It can be argued that all feelings are forms or intensities of these four basic ones. Each emotion listed here "feels" different from the others. By trying on each one, an individual can learn what feelings feel like, and can begin to experience naming and identifying inner reactions. From there, men can learn to identify deeper levels of nuance in their feelings and expand their emotional vocabularies. For example, they can learn the shades of difference between guilt and shame, anger and rage, satisfaction and joy.

It is important for men to learn that feelings do not always occur one at a time. For instance, anger is most often preceded by hurt, fear, or sadness—people get angry when they sense some sort of threat. Because anger is the only emotion allowed full expression in traditional masculinity, men often convert other feelings into anger. It is important for men to be able to identify the other feelings that gave rise to the anger. For example, a man may say that he feels angry when his wife spends an hour on the phone with her friends. A closer look may reveal sadness or hurt that his wife's attention is elsewhere. He may get angry when a prospective client rejects his sales pitch, but underlying that anger is a fear that he may lose his job because of poor performance. The expression of anger to the exclusion of other feelings limits the full range of emotional meanings and reactions.

Feelings are also accompanied by bodily sensations. Senses of tight muscles, a contorted face, a pounding heart, gooseflesh, or "butterflies in the stomach" are clues to emotional response. Our bodies and minds are directly connected. It is impossible to experience stress, anger, or other intense emotion and be completely physically relaxed at the same time. Therefore, body awareness can act as a gateway to emotional awareness. When one senses physical changes such as tight muscles, an upset stomach, a headache, or neck pain, it helps to first identify the thought or event that seemed to trigger the physical change, and to then try to identify the feelings that go with the bodily sensation.

Sometimes men who have been stripped of their expression of feelings for most of their lives have difficulty with these basic exercises. The experience of "I'm not good at this" may be frustrating or confusing. That is alright; it is a start. In fact, simply trying the exercises may lead one to feel sad or angry because it is so difficult. A person who has spent most of his life learning how not to feel is not expected to recover his emotional life in a moment. He must have empathy for himself as a person who struggles and be patient with a process that may be very slow.

HOW CAN MEN LEARN THE IMPORTANCE OF EXPRESSING FEELINGS?

The person who can say "I feel sad and angry because of what happened at work today" is less likely to express these feelings through disturbed behaviors or other symptoms than the person who simply enters the house and gets set off by the first thing that happens. When we can understand our feelings and reactions to events, we can choose our responses instead of acting emotions out through behavior or somatic symptoms.

An important additional effect of the appropriate expression of feelings is that this kind of communication is more likely to be understood and to get positive responses from others. For instance, when a man feels jealous because his wife's attention is not on him, he can do what men often do—convert his vulnerability into anger and confront her in accusatory tones. Doing so is likely to get a negative reaction from her—she may be acting in a very reasonable way, feel as if she is being attacked, and defend her actions. On the other hand, he could wait for an opportunity to tell her that he feels lonely or abandoned, and that he would like her help with these uncomfortable feelings. In this case, she might be more apt to comfort him because he has "owned" his vulnerability for himself and respectfully asked for her support. The conversion of vulnerability to jealousy and anger results in damage to the relationship. The acknowledgment and owning of vulnerable feelings results in a more cooperative and intimate relationship.

There are blocks to awareness of feelings for many men. We have reviewed the origins of these blocks in Chapters 2 and 3. How men overcome these blocks is as much a matter of skill and technique as it is an attitude toward oneself. After understanding the effects of family development and the socialization process, no man would blame another man for getting lost in the masculine dilemma or any of the other limitations of traditional masculinity. As we saw with Jack, when men give themselves the same empathy they would give another man, effective change begins to occur.

IS IDENTIFYING FEELINGS
THE SAME AS EMPATHY?

Identifying and naming feelings is a necessary, but not sufficient, condition for empathy. It is the first step in the process of coming to a full understanding of one's emotional life.

Empathy involves understanding another's feelings and thoughts. Empathy for the self is having compassion for the hurt and pain one feels in response to loss, conflicts, and failures associated with social shaming. It is almost like relating to the self as another person. Jack realized how developmental and socialization processes beyond his control resulted in his own pain and limited expressiveness. He was not the man, husband, and father he wanted to be. The reasons for this shortcoming were not all his doing. Having empathy for his own feelings allowed him to empathize with his wife's feelings. Jack was better able to attend to his wife's needs when he allowed himself to recognize and understand his own needs.

Men begin the process of expressing feelings through empathy. In our proposed treatment of masculine depression, empathy starts with the self and extends to others. Accurate empathy for self results in responsibility for changing the behavior that distorts men's real feelings.

WHAT HELPS MEN CHANGE THEIR VIEWS OF THEMSELVES?

There are several processes and habits to change here. One of them is accomplished simply by education and exposure to other ways of understanding men's development, such as the one that we are proposing. Another involves the three-step process of:

1. Separating from men's subjective experiences of shame and failure
2. Resisting the defensive stance of traditional masculinity
3. Accepting responsibility for change

Still another is taking time to validate and support oneself through a difficult change process. Jack had a lot of work in front of him. Rather than letting the enormity of this work discourage him, he allowed himself to appreciate the difficulty of the work and to appreciate himself for having the courage to try something so difficult and so different.

What Helps Men to Change the Way in Which They Present Themselves to Others?

Men can tap into the emotional life via an entryway that is quite natural for many men: storytelling. Talking with others about one's experiences is part and parcel of traditional masculinity. Usually, this activity involves telling a story in a colorful and entertaining way. Men often take turns doing so, and also frequently try to "top" the previous story. This is a competitive mode of storytelling, one that is not very useful for the purpose of developing empathy and sharing feelings. However, if one tells them a little differently, stories can be very useful.

With a trusted friend or with a group of men, try telling stories in which you were confronted with powerful emotions. Many of these may stem from childhood or adolescent experiences such as the ones we recounted in Chapter 3. Instead of telling these stories in the usual masculine mode, i.e., concentrating solely on events, take some time to identify and explore your emotional reactions to the events. Try to focus on the emotional content of the story rather than the event itself. When we were little boys, we were very adept at feeling. Through years of harsh socialization, we lost some of our ability to be emotional human beings. As adults, we learned that other men did not seem to want to hear about our emotional lives. With trusted confidants, story telling can help men recover some of the emotional wisdom we had as boys.

It took generations of patterns and a lifetime of learning to acquire the limitations of traditional masculinity. The effects of traditional masculinity are both obvious and subtle, and, as we saw in Chapter 3, quite pervasive. Men can and must learn to tolerate difficulties as a part of the process of changing their sense of what masculinity really means. After all, a man would allow someone else to make a mistake and not get it right the first time. A man would support and encourage another man's tackling a painful change of this magnitude and difficulty. Why not give the self the same tolerance, understanding, and support?

The following case study demonstrates many of the topics we have discussed in this chapter: dissociation, the masculine dilemma, empathy, and expression of feelings.

Brad's Story

Brad is a twenty-year-old college student whom I saw in the counseling center at a large university. He had come to school on a full academic scholarship to study particle physics, and his performance in school had been nearly perfect. When I saw him in the spring semester of his junior year, he had received only one "B" in his entire academic career, and that had been in a one-credit physical education course. He was doing research at the level of an advanced graduate student, had won several awards, and had demonstrated academic excellence in nearly every way imaginable. He was clearly on the fast track to a PhD and a career as a high-level researcher.

Brad came to the counseling center because he had been arrested by the campus police for peeping in the windows of the women's residence halls. In keeping with the university's conduct policy, he had been placed on probation, meaning that he would be suspended for a full year for any infraction within the subsequent year. He was required to attend counseling sessions as a condition of his probation.

Brad was certainly an atypical college student, but, in many ways, he was a typical sex offender—emotionally immature, and with a talent for deflecting any conversation about his problematic behavior. He presented the peeping incident to me as an unfortunate misunderstanding—he had just "happened" to be around the women's dormitories on a walk he was taking to get a break from studying (he stuck to this story despite a police report stating that several witnesses had said that he had looked into a particular window for more than fifteen minutes). Brad was quite friendly and superficially cooperative. He stated that he was quite willing to attend counseling sessions. In fact, he said, it was a good opportunity for him to work on his personal issues, which he assured me were ordinary ones.

Brad described his father as a cruel tyrant and his mother as an absolute saint. His childhood had been filled with a harsh discipline that amounted to emotional and sometimes physical abuse at the hands of his father. His mother was his only source of refuge from his pain until he met his girlfriend, whom he spoke of in the same glowing terms that he described his mother. They could do no wrong, as far as he was concerned. Neither his girlfriend nor his mother was even remotely capable of causing any sort of relationship difficulty, no matter how minor, even by mistake. When problems arose with his girlfriend, he always considered them his fault. He believed himself unworthy of being in a relationship with her, and he was both puzzled and eternally grateful that she would be with him. Brad described both his turbulent relationship with his father and his wonderful relationships with his girlfriend and his mother in highly intellectualized fashion—there was little, if any, real feeling in any of his conversation. He was the stereotypical scientist, viewing emotions as a nuisance or an unnecessary distraction.

Therapy with Brad was slow going. He was a well-defended client, and despite his statements (and perhaps even beliefs) to the contrary, he had little or no personal investment in the counseling process. But that had changed by our fourth meeting. The night before his appointment, Brad had once again been caught by the campus police peering into the windows of women's residence hall rooms. He was almost surely going to be suspended, and he foresaw the dream of his future career going up in smoke. He was absolutely distraught. No longer able to deflect his feelings by intellectualizing, his state of acute distress provided a therapeutic window of opportunity—a chance for him to learn something about himself that he could not learn in his usual highly defended state. His wounds were open, allowing him to see inside of them.

I asked Brad to close his eyes, envision what had happened the night before, and tell me about the incident as if it were happening in the present moment. I asked him to use the present tense in all of his descriptions, and to tell me the entire story of the whole evening in as much detail as he could remember. In one of the most powerful therapy sessions in which I have ever taken part, he told the story in enough detail to nearly fill the entire therapy hour. As Brad recalled them, the series of events were as follows:

Early that evening, Brad's girlfriend had told him that she was sexually attracted to his best friend. Although she and Brad were engaged, she told him that she wondered if maybe his best friend was actually "the one" for her, and she felt that she owed it to herself and to him to find out. So, she told Brad that she wanted to have sex with his best friend (!) so that she would not make the mistake of marrying Brad if he, in fact, was not "the one." Because of his lack of emotional and relationship sophistication, and because of his overidealization of his girlfriend, Brad had quickly convinced himself that his girlfriend's proposal was a reasonable one. (Fortunately, Brad's friend later refused to participate in this "experiment" as he understood how much harm it would bring for all concerned.)

Brad had convinced himself intellectually that his girlfriend's plan made sense, as he believed that she was infallible. As was his habit, he had dissociated himself from his emotional pain. He was obviously very skilled at dissociation—he was even able to do it within a few minutes after the woman he loved told him that she was going to have sex with his best friend.

Later that evening, Brad was studying, and at some point, he felt a little bit tired. He decided to take a break and, as is his habit, to take a short walk outside in order to refresh himself. At that point, according to Brad's account, he "zoned out." He was only vaguely aware of himself, his body, or the route that he was taking on his walk. The next thing he remembered was the police interrupting him at the window of a women's residence hall. As in the first incident, he had been there some fifteen or twenty minutes, but he could not recall how he got there or even what he had seen through the window.

Brad had undergone a distinct dissociative episode. His interaction with his girlfriend had brought him considerable emotional pain, but he was unable to acknowledge it because of his highly intellectual-ized style and his view of her as incapable of human faults. The peeping incidents were his indirect way of acting out his anger toward her and compensating for his underlying sense of masculine inadequacy. In a way, he was symbolically being unfaithful to her by viewing other women in some stage of undress (an expression of his anger), and he was overpowering a victim by watching her without her knowledge or permission. In this way, he was compensating for feelings of powerlessness—which, like all feelings, he could not ac-knowledge to himself.

Through further painstaking therapeutic work, Brad came to under-stand that he *did* have feelings, that these feelings were important, and that conflict was a normal part of any relationship. He learned how to deal with his girlfriend in a more direct manner—to sometimes feel angry with her, to express his anger directly and appropriately, to disagree with her, and to negotiate with her. Instead of passively fol-lowing along with whatever she said (and then passive-aggressively acting out his anger), he found his own voice in the relationship. Having learned how to recognize his feelings and give himself permis-sion to have them, he had learned to have empathy for himself. He became happier, and his relationship with his girlfriend improved considerably.

Men who consistently, habitually, and systematically squelch their feelings for long periods of time eventually cease to feel altogether. When they do, they lose their points of reference for understanding the feelings of others, and they become dehumanized. Empathy for the self is gone, and thus empathy for the other has become impossible. Empathy for self does not result in self-indulgence. When a man recovers his emotional experience, it becomes possible to access the emotional experiences of others and have satisfying and intimate relationships. Appropriate empathy for the self leads to acceptance of the responsibility for changing destructive behaviors.

WHAT ARE THE ABCs OF CHANGE?

Affect
  —Learn a language for feelings.
  —Learn to feel for yourself as well as for others.

Behavior
  —Try on new words and meanings.
  —Learn how to support and encourage yourself.
  —Work at understanding the pain behind your own mask so that you can develop empathy for others.

Cognition
  —Give yourself a break.
  —Remind yourself that you are not to blame for growing into these problems.
  —Destructive behaviors do not mean that you are flawed, bad, or a failure. They do mean that you are responsible for changing them.

Chapter 6

Relation to Other Men

I had the privilege of leading an ongoing men's therapy group. Several sets of men had cycled through and improved. They were more clear about their career goals, and those who struggled with alcohol problems had achieved stable sobriety. Many group members reported an improvement in their general mood and outlook. When each man left the group, he was able to say what he had gained through the group experience. In general, I felt good about the therapeutic experience that being in the group gave to these men. It is still surprising to me that an experience as simple as talking openly and honestly to other men can be so healing.

One particular group of men had been together for about nine months. There was something different about this group. They had jelled. Their love for one another was alive, and they expressed it directly. They believed in one another and did not hesitate to say so. The accepting environment of the group allowed these men to face failures and shortcomings with the same honesty as successes and strengths. Rather than shaming or poking fun at one another, as men (ironically, in a misguided attempt to make things better) so often do, they supported one another's efforts to match their behaviors to their intentions. They moved beyond the good-natured teasing of the locker room into an honest sharing of feelings.

Greg was the newest member, having been with the group for only two months. He had not quite "joined" yet. He tried to "talk the talk," but something was missing. The group stayed with him, giving him time to get used to them. They understood that it is difficult to join a group when the emphasis is on talking from the heart. Men usually have more experience with joining groups such as athletic teams, where the emphasis is almost solely on performance.

During one session, Greg was trying to tell the group about the pain that he felt in his failing marriage, but his words seemed empty. He was stuck, wanting their support but feeling unable to ask for it. He fell into an awkward silence, and the rest of the group also remained quiet. I knew his history and the full extent of his marital problems. I knew that he was not letting them know how bad he felt. I could not "rescue" him and say it for him, so I decided to let the silence unfold. While I was wondering what to do next, Jim leaped up, grabbed Greg out of his chair, pulled him to the floor, and proceeded to have a wrestling and tickling match with him. They laughed like brothers. After five or ten minutes, Greg got up off the floor, sat in his chair, and finally began to pour out how empty and lost he felt. He was terrified that he would reach inside himself and find nothing there. He had tried to maintain an image of happiness and competence with his wife, but it was not meaningful. She felt his emotional absence and planned to leave. He felt like a failure, and his shame was overwhelming. He poured out stories about an emotionally distant father whom he could not please. Greg felt inadequate as a man and he was overwhelmed by shame and doubt. He related how he had made it through childhood and adolescence on his own, never letting anyone know how empty he felt. (This is a common experience for many boys.)

Through all of Greg's story, this group of men listened . . . and loved. Their presence, understanding, and acceptance were profound. They knew from their own struggles just how he felt. Each man gave Greg his full attention, eye contact, and understanding words. In this group, Greg had the unique and unmistakable experience of being in relationship with men who said "we understand you, we accept you, we love you." He began the process of reclaiming himself that night. He was accepted *by men*. His value as a person was affirmed and validated *by men*.

Greg did not just think or feel the acceptance of the group, he *knew* it. It was as real as Jim's physical connection with him. Had Greg only *thought* that he was accepted, he would not have been able to open up and share his inner struggle. Had he only *felt* accepted, his history of feeling unaccepted would have quickly overcome this new feeling. But, he *knew* that he was accepted. There was something visceral in Jim's connection with him that allowed him to experience an acceptance by men. From there, Greg could begin to fill and transform the chronic emptiness that had haunted him for most of his life.

The main therapeutic intervention for Greg was Jim's wrestling connection. There was nothing for me, as the therapist, to say. These two men were connecting to and healing each other. Jim's behavior said to Greg, "You are a man—one of us; we accept and affirm your value as a man." When the time came for Greg to leave the group, he could not express with words what he had received from the other men in the group. His behavior and relationships with men and women had changed immeasurably.

I had known Eric for a few months. We lived in the same community and had several opportunities to talk with each other. We knew each other's professions and families. Our children played together, and we used those times to get to know each other and reminisce about growing up in simpler times. At a community picnic, we had a chance to sit and have a hot dog together. He asked about my areas of professional specialization. Wanting to continue developing the friendship, I told him that one of my specialties is the treatment of survivors of severe trauma. I shared with him how intense and at times painful the work is. I told him of my sense of social obligation to do this work and a spiritual commitment not to let someone's suffering go unrecognized and untreated. I told him how this work always pushed me to the limits of my training and how vulnerable I felt at times. Eric listened. When I paused he asked, "Can I get you some potato salad?" I felt a gathering shame. I knew I had violated the unspoken but sacred rule that men should never talk about vulnerable feelings, connections to other people, or anything else except sports, women, and money. Part of me wished that I could take back what I had revealed, not as much the information I had conveyed to him, but my feelings and emotional investment in the issue. Eric's response let me know how far I had strayed from "men's talk." Although I later found some humor in the interaction, I also found a basic sense of shame in my gender role violation.

HOW ARE TRADITIONAL MASCULINITY AND MASCULINE DEPRESSION CONNECTED TO MEN'S RELATIONSHIPS WITH ONE ANOTHER?

It is in the gaze of other men that destructive masculinity is constructed and sustained. Not surprisingly, it is also in relationships with men that this gaze is broken. The fear of attack and the loss of credibility in the male community drive men to perform, succeed, and avoid the display of emotions. Men want to be socially accepted, so they conform to the masculine norms that they learned throughout socialization. The unstated goal is to be seen as a "real man" by other men. Ironically, men are supposed to be very independent and think for themselves, but a great many men almost robotically conform to masculine role demands. Whether it is an internalized locker room chorus, a male-driven corporate world, or a group of guys poking fun at one another, male relationships govern masculine behavior. It is from this real or imagined male community that approval for being male comes. It is within this same community that real change begins.

Traditional masculinity is destructive to women when—consciously or unconsciously—women are used to create this illusion of manliness. A beautiful wife or a wife who behaves like the "little woman" are familiar examples of ways that men have used women to maintain their masculine image with other men. Traditionally, both men and women have sought out healing from women, who are raised and encouraged to love, listen, understand, and be compassionate. Men tend to bring their emotional wounds to women because doing so with men feels unsafe. Because emotional disclosure, intimacy, and vulnerability are socially defined as unmasculine, men who display these qualities with other men risk rejection and/or neglect. It feels terrible to be hurting, tell someone about the pain, and meet with the typical masculine reactions: changing the subject, belittling or denying the pain, saying "Get over it," "Here's what you should do . . . ," or, in my case, "Can I get you some potato salad?" It feels safer for most men to talk with women when they want to express their feelings because men are more likely to get a comforting response from women.

Relationships with women can help men heal and grow, but because traditional masculinity is largely formed by and sustained in relationships with males, we believe that there is a special kind of healing that also comes in the context of these relationships. To free themselves from the impossible demands of traditional masculinity, they need to be able to feel safe from attack by other boys and men when they choose to behave in nontraditional ways. Men must learn to take the risk of revealing themselves to other men, and men must be validated, not attacked, for taking such a risk.

When men find support, understanding, and acceptance in the gaze of other men, the fear of attack is greatly diminished, and there is no need for masculine defense and bravado. It is in relation to other men that a real and unique opportunity for change exists. Greg changed because of the messages of Jim and the other group members—messages that spoke to relationship, acceptance, and common understanding.

Men are the ones who must change traditional masculinity. It is through healthy relationships that meaningful change occurs. While relationships with women are healing and life giving, the male relationship has a unique potential for healing some of the more entrenched and destructive aspects of traditional masculinity.

ISN'T THIS WHAT THE "MEN'S MOVEMENT" TRIED TO DO—CONNECT MEN TO OTHER MEN?

Not exactly. The mythopoetic men's movement of Robert Bly and his followers was not entirely successful because it was too restrictive. Men would go off on all-male weekends and then return to wives and families. The activities of these weekends did not connect them as much to one another as to a common masculinity via rituals that were designed to raise the "male spirit." Masculinity was explored out of its everyday context, and so it was very difficult to integrate this (supposedly) essential male spirit into existing relationships with women. Traditional men already have plenty of rituals in sports, work, clubs, lodges, and other historically male enclaves that take them away from family and real relationships. While the mythopoetic movement offered "better" (more spiritually significant) rituals, it did not emphasize enough men's needs to form direct intimate connections with each other. It was a step up from the primitive male bonding of a strip club or fraternity to a more sophisticated and spiritual essence, but it was still highly ritualized, and still a form of traditional "male bonding"— a process of connecting around an object or activity. Traditional men bond around sports, work, and the denigration of women. Mythopoetic men bond around ritual and a shared vision of essential masculinity. We believe that the men's movement needs the next step—direct relationships with other men. (We should also note here that many theorists reject the notion of essential and inborn masculinity, preferring instead to focus on the social forces that mold men's behavior and the common ground of human needs that unites, not separates, men and women.)

WHAT DO MEN REALLY NEED FROM OTHER MEN?

Friendship. Genuine friendships with other men are vital components to breaking the cycle of traditional masculinity. Friendship builds trust, expresses caring and support, and is based on a basic belief in the goodness of both people. As the opposite of the socialized aggression and defensiveness that breeds traditional masculinity, friendship allows growth through acceptance, emotional safety, and human caring.

It is important to make a distinction between authentic friendship and the kinds of relationships that most men have with each other, which many men's studies scholars are now referring to as "buddyships." A friend is somebody with whom you can share feelings and inner experiences, express caring in a direct way, and talk with about personal struggles and difficulties. A buddy is somebody you "bond with" through a third object or activity. While buddyships can be enjoyable and somewhat affirming, the person whose relationships are exclusively of this nature will lead a solitary life, never knowing another person or being known in any real sense.

Many men do not have friends or even acquaintances, and so they frequently lead isolated lives, even within their families. Many men lack a close male friend with whom to talk, celebrate successes, or air personal conflicts. In Greg's case, there was nobody to talk to, and the absence of a male friend made things worse for him. He had only himself to try to make sense of his feelings. Isolation rarely heals emotional pain of this type. Greg replicated the distant and negative messages he had received from his father. Unconsciously, he treated himself as he imagined that his father would—disapprovingly. The unhealthy relationship with a man, his father, had strongly influenced the development of Greg's problems. Therefore, the healthy relationships with other men effectively changed Greg's feelings about himself. This healing process made it possible for him to change his relationships with both women and men.

Increasingly, men want these close relationships with other men but feel reluctant to state this need openly because of the same traditional masculinity that creates this isolation. It is the "Catch 22" situation of men's emotional health. Greg wanted the group's acceptance and understanding, but he did not know how to ask for it. Jim spoke a language that opened a door for Greg. It was a visceral message that words could not convey. Jim's communication went beyond thoughts and feelings, and allowed Greg to develop meaningful relationships with men. Jim broke the pattern that had kept Greg stuck in his isolation.

WHY ARE RELATIONSHIPS WITH OTHER MEN SO VITAL TO THE HEALING PROCESS IN MEN?

As we argued in Chapter 2, a frequent outcome for men of family development is a core sense of inadequacy and anxiety. The original source of this anxiety is in relationship to an absent or emotionally distant father. Boys do not see the full range of their fathers' feelings or understand that being a man can be complex and difficult. It is in the absence of a role model who validates and leads the way that boys' fear of inadequacy begins. Therefore, it is in the presence of other men that healing and recovery occur in adulthood.

Numerous "unspoken messages" haunt men. The inner "locker room chorus" echoes in every man's mind in the form of the punishing messages of the socialization process that are comprised of male voices. Relationships with men can change this locker room chorus message from "you're a 'sissy' if you feel . . ." to "we also feel . . . ; you are okay."

As we noted before, it is impossible for men to develop a healthy identity based on the negative, e.g., "being not female." In relationships with other men, men develop an identity based on the positive, "I am being a whole person." When men fully share their true selves—their feelings, successes, doubts, achievements, and losses— with each other, men grow in health. Without this level of real sharing between men, they are left to fill in the blanks of "being not female" with myths, media images, and other distorted conceptions of masculinity.

When I talked with Eric that day, I heard my own locker room chorus. In fact, I hear it every time I sit down to write this book. Talking about men's insecurities indeed! I see and hear "the guys"

I went to school with, and I still fear their contempt for my betrayal of the brotherhood. We did not have a common definition of what being male really meant. In the absence of a positive definition, we bonded in the way that most boys and men do: "don't show me yours and I won't show you mine." It is possible for men to recognize, validate, and "reassociate" feelings, desires, and traits in each other. Jim knew Greg's unspoken pain. He was comfortable with his own feelings and helped Greg to find his. As men feel more confident and validated with feelings and complex conflicts, they become more capable of helping other men, and doing so furthers their own healing. Rather than producing and presenting fully formed and fully resolved opinions in a traditionally masculine way, as Greg was attempting to do, men can feel comfortable being more tentative and working out feelings and opinions in the context of relationships with other people. This cooperative style is often associated with the "feminine" management or relational style. We prefer to think of it as simply being human.

Changes such as these will soften men's basic isolation and transform fear-based masculine identity. Healthy masculine identity does not mean that men stop working hard, competing, pushing the limits of science and physical endurance, and achieving professionally. Too often men fear that change will be associated with a loss of power. It is precisely this fear that serves to maintain the status quo. However, a healthy masculine identity is not a loss; it is an *expansion*. It incorporates the joys of accomplishment within a larger picture of self, relationships, and community. Men become more sophisticated and aware of a relationship context that they have ignored for most of their lives. Developing in this way can often help them in the working world.

HOW DO TRADITIONAL RELATIONSHIPS WITH OTHER MEN MAINTAIN THE PROBLEM?

As discussed in Chapter 3, males are punished more severely than females for gender role violations, and it is primarily other males that deliver this punishment. Whether it is in the form of an internalized "locker room chorus" or overt rejections and shaming, the real or imagined resistance to adult male change in behavior comes primarily from men. In simple terms, men keep men from changing. Traditional masculinity has prevented men from having intimate relationships. Men learn this behavioral style in order to defend themselves from the attacks of other men. The threat involved with behaving in unmasculine ways becomes internalized, so that the man defends himself from "feminine" experiences, even when other men are not around. In their masculine posturing, men implicitly say to each other, "Let me stay behind my defenses and I'll let you stay behind yours," and "I won't attack you if you don't attack me." Although he probably didn't realize it, Eric's response was loud and clear. I had talked about feeling alone and unsure of myself. I had betrayed the brotherhood. Doing so created a sense of masculine anxiety for him, and so he abruptly changed the subject to feel safe. In adulthood, other men maintain the "locker room chorus" and the reminders to "act like a man."

When other men do not accept or initiate meaningful change in masculinity, there is a basic reinforcement of the traditional masculine stance. No change is perceived as no need to change. If men continue to behave in traditionally masculine ways, it is considered the right thing to do.

WHAT DO MEN HAVE TO OFFER ONE ANOTHER?

Men can validate the feelings, conflicts, and needs that have been dissociated from awareness. Once these needs and feelings are accepted as valid and real, they do not need to be dissociated or acted out. Men can give one another the message that feelings, conflicts, and needs are a part of men's experience and that a man can be fully human without losing his masculinity. Greg did not simply hear that message, he experienced it at a core level. The limiting effects of traditional masculinity are softened when the initial recognition of and acceptance of feelings takes place in the company of men, who can identify with one another and find refuge from the unrealistic demands of traditional masculinity.

Since men are socialized similarly in our culture, men are more likely to understand and recognize the unnamed conflicts, joys, and struggles involved in masculine development. Men can recognize for one another the desires and intentions to be fully human. For instance, men can recognize that men want to be good fathers. Women and children who experience a man's angry temperament may not be as aware of this (understandably so, as their experience of fear is overwhelming at times). The man may know that he has lost his way and is acting like his father. His behavior hurts those around him and only perpetuates the destructiveness associated with masculinity. These psychological issues may be difficult to see for the family who faces a stern and unyielding tyrant, or for the spouse who tries to interact with a distant, aloof, and underinvolved man.

Men's original desire to love or be loved can become distorted through masculine depression. It is difficult for others to see the pain behind the mask of dangerous and destructive behaviors. Healing can occur when men recognize for one another that conflicts are really difficult and confusing. Behind the mask of a workaholic and seemingly successful father/husband, deep needs and emotional pain often exist.

There are no excuses for the destructive behaviors that men display, but there is responsible change. Meaningful change can begin in relation to other men and in the eyes of other men. They can hold one another responsible for destructive behavior in a way that women and the legal system cannot. The following true story illustrates the process of masculine destructiveness and the possibility for change.

The Washington Post recently ran a story about a northern Virginia country club that held an event called the "Vodka Challenge." It was a men-only event, a standard country club golf tournament. What made it newsworthy was the mode of celebration in the men's locker room. The day before the tournament, one of the club managers had arranged for an ice sculpture to be made. It was a sculpture of a nude woman, sitting down with her legs spread. The vodka was served in the locker room from a fountain stream that came out from between her legs.

When some of the female club members found out about this ice sculpture, they were understandably outraged. Most of the men seemed to react with puzzlement. After all, this was a sculpture, not a real woman, and it was in the men's locker room, where none of the women would even see it. Predictably, there were a lot of statements about angry feminists who have no sense of humor, and the overly rigid atmosphere of political correctness.

If men were able to let down their defenses, they would see that, symbolically, the ice sculpture provided an atmosphere that says,

"Women are here for men's pleasure, and we will bond around our shared masculinity in this place where we don't have to deal with women as human beings." Seeing women as lower-status people who are not like us, and who therefore don't deserve as much respect, allows men to justify mistreating them in many ways, including violence. There is an attitudinal undercurrent of women as enemies, in spite of the fact that most of these men were attached to and raising children (including, for many, daughters) with one of these enemies.

We can find other informal men's groups in any workplace, college dorm, athletic team, and corner bar, telling demeaning jokes about women, calling them by animal names or the names of their genitals. These men *rarely* confront one another for fear of being attacked or ostracized for singing notes that are dissonant with the "locker room chorus," which in this case, literally took place in a locker room.

We have no doubt that, in the locker room at the Vodka Challenge, there was at least one man who was uncomfortable with this ice sculpture, just as when someone hires a stripper for a bachelor party or makes a woman the butt of a joke. It is likely that *more* than one man felt that way. But nobody spoke up because each man felt that he was the only one, and taking on the collective opinion of the rest of the group could leave him out in the cold, ostracized from the others and perhaps ridiculed as an unmasculine "pantywaist mama's boy." It would have taken tremendous courage for a man to stand up and say, "That ice sculpture is disgusting; what could you have been thinking? Can't you see what this does to our mothers and sisters and wives, not to mention our own reputations? Why don't we just get rid of it before we're all embarrassed? We can have fun without ridiculing women." Ironically, while courage is supposed to be a hallmark of traditional masculinity, many men find it impossible to exhibit this kind of courage. They would sooner run into a burning building or have a fist fight.

Social psychologists have known for a long time that unanimity within a group is one of the biggest barriers to being able to disagree. When the group opinion is unanimous and you do not have an ally, the pressure to conform is tremendous. *But*, if even one person voices a disagreement with the rest of the group, others are much more likely to follow suit.[1] There were probably several uncomfortable men in that locker room that day. If one of them had spoken out, he might have found that there was more support in the room than he had imagined.

But somebody has to go first. Somebody has to take a risk. It is masculine to take a risk, but men have to learn to expand the notions of appropriate courage and risk taking into the realm of the emotional and interpersonal. Greg found out that there could be tremendous gain from taking this kind of risk. Although my risk taking with Eric met with less enthusiasm, I am committed to continuing to affirm my humanity in relationships with other men. Who knows? Perhaps Eric changed a little bit from that interaction, but he was too uncomfortable to stay with the feeling.

HOW CAN AN INEXPERIENCED MAN FORM AN AUTHENTIC FRIENDSHIP WITH ANOTHER MAN?

In recent years, many men are discovering that their relationships with other men are emotionally impoverished. They want a deeper connection, but they do not know how to establish one. Following are a few simple step-by-step instructions that may be useful. They are mainly gleaned from an *Utne Reader* article by Larry Letich in which he describes "guerilla tactics for making a friend."[2] He uses this title to acknowledge that society conspires against genuine male friendships, and so to form one, you have to be rather subversive (although the war metaphor is unfortunate in this context).

1. First, you have to want it. Identify for yourself the benefits that true friendship can bring. Remind yourself that you are not strange, unmasculine, or unhealthy because you want a friend. In fact, being able to recognize your need for a friend and commit to establishing a friendship is a sign of health, openness, and personal growth.
2. Identify someone who might be a potential friend. Seek someone who seems to want to question the values of traditional masculinity.
3. Find some way to spend some time with this man. Initially, having coffee or a beer, or doing some activity together is a good way to become involved in a comfortable and low-pressure way.

4. Try to make honest, personal conversation in an appropriate time frame and context.
5. If you are successful in achieving a connection with this man, at some point, talk about your friendship with him and express to him that you care about him and value your time together.

Friendships proceed at a certain pace, and going too fast or too slow can be detrimental. You don't "bare your soul" to someone you hardly know, but you don't spend hours talking about trivialities, either. Keep in mind that, for most men, the establishment of a real friendship is an *effortful* undertaking, even though the *desire* for closeness and connection is entirely natural. Also keep in mind that developing and maintaining friendships requires *skills*, and that skills improve with practice. Feeling awkward is more the rule than the exception (as with any skill—remember the first time you swung a golf club, played a musical instrument, made a presentation, etc.?). The goal is not to wait until you feel comfortable; it is to try to establish the friendship *despite* feeling a little bit uncomfortable. As with any skill, comfort comes when you start to get better at it.

HOW CAN RELATIONSHIPS WITH MEN CHANGE MEN'S DEPENDENCY ON WOMEN?

Greg did not know it, but he had made the standard and the impossible request of his wife—"fix me." This is a standard request because men carry unresolved issues about identity and masculinity into adulthood, and these unresolved issues are usually unavoidable in intimate relationships. It is an impossible request because the source of the problem is embedded in relationships with men. This part of traditional masculinity cannot be resolved in a relationship with a woman.

Greg was not the only one in the group who experienced radical change. It was easy and natural for a man to listen and love in this group because other group members had experienced profound change. There was common ground. Like Greg, other group members also had relationships with women that were their only source of genuine human contact. In the absence of real friendships with males, men turn to women to fulfill their emotional needs. Even though the dilemma of "not too close, not too far away" can prevent an emotionally satisfying relationship, it is often the only real relationship in a man's life. As a result, these solitary relationships take on a kind of inner intensity for men that is not healthy.

Greg's process of strongly connecting with the group continued. He was able to explore his inner self with other men. This process helped Greg become more comfortable with his feelings and reactions. He began to understand himself, trust himself, and allow himself to interact with other people instead of putting on a show of false confidence. He learned to feel more comfortable with just being Greg. He was no longer dependent on others to provide him with comfort and approval, as he had begun to find these things for himself. His relationships with women transformed. No longer did he turn to women with the impossible request. He began to bring a substance, a stronger sense of self, to his relationships with women. There was true interaction between equals. Gone was the paradoxical dominance of traditional masculinity, in which a man assumes the role of head of the house but secretly relies on a woman to make him feel like a man. Greg was accepted in the eyes of the men in his life who mattered. He brought this validation into his relationships with women. He was free to love, trust, and engage. He was no longer haunted and dominated by unspoken fears.

When men heal men, relationships with women can also change. Men and women can enter relationships based on desire rather than deficiencies. This kind of relationship is interactive and mutually enhancing, not fear-based and struggling for power. "I like how she adds to my life and actively choose to be with her" is different from "I can't live without her." In more dependent relationships, women frequently say "it's like having another child to take care of." Men who have resolved their childhood issues around gender demands no longer remain trapped in that childhood.

WHAT ARE THE ABCs OF CHANGE?

Affect
　　　—making connections with other men creates anxiety. Expect to feel uncomfortable and learn to manage this feeling. Anxiety is an indication that something very important is going on. It is not a reason to stop.

Behavior
  —Make a friend. Talking to a friend is different than just "shooting the breeze."

Cognition
  —use self-talk: "This is important to me," "I can do this," and "Skills improve with practice."

Chapter 7

Relation to Women

Intimate relationships are difficult, complex, and often problematic. Volumes have been written about this subject, and our purpose is not to reinvent the wheel by redefining the character of all intimate relationships. Rather, our focus in this chapter is to apply the basic model of masculine depression to intimate relationships with women. Dissociated feelings and destructive behavior impair these relationships in predictable ways. *Empathy for one's partner* is one of the most powerful antidotes to masculine depression.

A relationship is a *connection* between people. Among other characteristics, intimate relationships require two basic qualities:

- revealing and sharing the self (talking about feelings), and
- accurate understanding and respect for the other person's perspectives and feelings (empathy).

Traditional masculinity tends to develop the opposites of these qualities. Even when men share their own feelings, they can still have difficulty understanding and accepting another person's feelings. Masculine development builds *masters*, but intimate relationships are made of *mates*.

Fred's Problem

Fred had been in therapy for two months, basically because his wife was on the verge of leaving him. He loved her very much, and could not envision life without her. They had two children, a nice house, and an active social life. He was the prototype of the successful male—he had a lucrative career, was athletic, handsome, and young, and was married to a beautiful woman. From all outward appearances, he had it all. Few of his friends knew how desperate the situation at home had become. His wife avoided all opportunities to be with him. She had gone so far as to tell him that she did not love him and was not sure she ever would again. Over the years Fred had neglected his kids, disregarded his wife's needs, and generally ran his life exactly as he pleased. His wife finally rebelled and withdrew from the marriage. In response he had tried to change. He was home on time, spent more time with the kids, found ways to be happy without her, and did not pressure her for time, sex, or a promise to stay with him. Yet she continued to avoid him and was angry at what seemed to him to be insignificant things. He was feeling quite despondent. It seemed that things were never going to get better.

Earlier in therapy, Fred had been reactive and defensive. He found it difficult to listen to his wife without discarding her views as incorrect, especially when they differed from his views. Fred based his actions on his own thoughts, needs, and perspectives. If he thought that something was a good idea, he did it, regardless of how it involved and affected other people. After all, he knew that he had only good intentions. Fred had never stopped to think about how others felt or were affected by his behaviors. I asked him, "Who else in your family operates in this way?" His face fell. He and his wife had often engaged in long arguments about how intrusive and controlling his grandmother was. He had always defended his grandmother in these fights. Now it startled him to see that he was unintentionally doing the same thing. He slowly saw a pattern emerging. He had "run over" his wife with his own thoughts, desires, and solutions to problems. There was no room in the marriage for her thoughts and desires. Now she avoided any contact with him. One of the things that provoked this avoidance was the way in which he reacted to her when she was angry with him—he did everything that he could to get her to stop being angry. She felt that this reaction denied her feelings and made her feel guilty for being angry.

For instance, he was in a meeting and knew that he should have stopped briefly to call to let her know that he was going to be late. He did not, fearing that doing so would make him appear unmasculine in front of his male co-workers. When he arrived home thirty minutes late, she said that she was angry because once again work was more important to him than she was. He felt a sudden rush of anxiety. His first instinct was to defend himself and blame her for being inflexible.

He resisted this urge (as we had worked on previously in therapy). But he was still "scrambling" and not sure what to do. He left the room to collect his thoughts and returned to say that she was right and that in the future he would not do it again. Fred was surprised that this statement did not soothe his wife. Without saying why, she became more angry and felt like withdrawing more. He was confused.

I asked Fred to go back to the moment when she first said that she was angry. What did he feel in that instant? It took him a while to reexperience the event. As he did, he felt overwhelming fear, discomfort, and rising panic. He was scared to death of her anger and was doing anything he could to stop her from feeling what she was feeling. He never apologized for what he had done because he feared that doing so might support her anger, the very thing that he was trying to avoid. Rather, he said that it would never happen again. Fred expected her to say that everything was forgiven and that she was no longer angry. She didn't. Now he could see how his response had only made the situation worse. He was too uncomfortable to allow her to be angry. She needed to be free in the relationship to feel her own feelings, including her occasional anger. Given their unhealthy relationship pattern, it was easy to see why she felt that she had lost herself and her feelings for him.

As he understood that moment of anxiety, he saw how he had helped to create the conflict his wife had experienced. However, this insight did not resolve the problem for him. He remained bewildered. If he did not take her feelings away from her, he was lost. He asked me quite pointedly, "What else could I do?" I asked him what he felt when he did not know how to handle this situation. He said he felt very uncomfortable, anxious, and afraid. I asked him if his wife knew this. He just looked at me. In the silence he understood. Of course she did not know, because he had never told her. In fact he had never let either his wife—or even himself—see this part of him. When she felt angry, he felt out of control, vulnerable, and lost. All of the masculine training and masculine successes in his life did not prepare him for that moment. Traditional masculinity led Fred to fear that his wife's anger meant that he was a failure as a man. For his marriage to survive, Fred had to come to terms with his fear of his wife's feelings (as discussed in Chapters 2 and 4), and move beyond his traditional masculine identity, which was based on control and on being the master of things in his life (as explored in Chapters 3 and 6).

We talked more about what that moment really meant. If he allowed his wife to have her feelings, he would have to face his own feelings instead of scrambling to avoid the discomfort he felt in the face of hers. Fred and I had previously talked about the masculine dilemma in relationships. He felt it now. He knew how raw and vulnerable he would feel if he were to express his feelings to his wife. He also knew how difficult it was for him to have empathy for his wife's struggle. Fred knew more about his feelings than hers. He was frightened by her feelings and had used his masculine bullying behaviors to protect himself. His defensiveness kept Fred from having empathy for her and understanding for what she had been trying to tell him for years. The only hope for Fred to save his marriage lay in his developing an understanding of his own emotional world and an empathy for that of his wife. He had to grow into being a mate, not a master. If he could not do so, he would lose his wife.

*   *   *

As stated in Chapter 6, men cannot prove or maintain their masculinity through women. Because other men have not usually been sources of healing, men have tended to bring their psychological injuries, doubts, and fears with them into relationships with women. But men have not often presented these negative experiences to women in direct ways, e.g., "I feel depressed today, honey; the boss yelled at me and everything I touch seems to fail. I wonder if I'm cut out for this." Instead these troubles have been translated into the traditionally masculine behaviors of emotional avoidance and destructiveness. Women cannot carry the sole responsibility for healing and socializing men. Men need to overcome the effects of masculine development and develop better relational skills.

Too often, women's burden of affirming men has come at the cost of their own freedom to grow as individuals. In Fred's case, the damage was in the subtle way he asked his wife to maintain his masculinity by not being angry with him. Her anger meant he had failed as a man and as a husband. If he had been "doing it right," she would not be angry. The paradox is that, without being freely able to feel her anger, she could not have any other feelings for him either. The more he tried the traditional masculine way of controlling and fixing it, the worse the situation became. In time, Fred had become more able to express his feelings to her. The next critical step was learning to have *empathy* for *her* feelings.

WHAT IS EMPATHY?

Simply stated, empathy is an accurate emotional understanding of another person's thoughts, feelings, and desires. Empathy allows the internal experience of one person to make sense to another. When a man can truly say, "I understand; if I were you, I would think and feel the same way," empathy has been achieved. Too often, men do not understand women because men have dissociated from their own feelings and thus have no point of reference for identifying with women's emotional reactions. In the absence of empathy, many men blame their wives or partners for having reactions that they do not understand. Empathy allows cooperation to replace an adversarial relationship with a partner.

Empathy is an absolute necessity for a healthy relationship, and several elements must be present in order for empathy to develop. The first precondition of empathy is a basic level of trust in the relationship. It is a risk to expose one's vulnerability to another person, and a kind of interpersonal safety has to exist to do so. For some couples, emotional "scar tissue" from years of conflict has eroded this sense of psychological safety, and they have to make serious efforts to recover it for the relationship to survive.

A second precondition of empathy is the emotional disclosure of one partner to another. Fred wanted his wife's empathy, but he never told her how he felt. In fact, Fred himself rarely paid attention to his feelings. Men often have difficulty receiving empathy because of low self-disclosure; it is very difficult to identify with someone's feelings when he or she does not reveal these feelings. Women are often adept at self-disclosure, but they frequently do not receive their partner's empathy because men often lack the skills for attending to their feelings, having been raised in a world where the head is always defined as more important than the heart. As a result of these emotional misunderstandings, many couples find themselves engaged in frequent power struggles to work out whose needs will be addressed in which order.

The third precondition is a motivational one. Individuals must make sincere efforts to attend to and identify with their partners' feelings. The man must learn to listen for emotional themes in his partner's communication instead of becoming defensive and attempting to re-assert his dominance. He has to move from saying, "Here's why your reactions are wrong . . ." to saying, "Help me to understand your reactions so that we can work together to deal with our differences." The so-called "battle of the sexes" is not inevitable. When couples cooperate with each other instead of jockeying for psychological posi-tion, "battles" evolve into adjustments and teamwork. Couples must learn how to recognize power struggles and transform them into prob-lems that they can work on together.

WHAT DO MEN NEED TO DEVELOP EMPATHY FOR THEIR PARTNERS?

We emphasize two basic qualities for men:

- talking about your own feelings, and
- listening actively and focusing on your partner in an attempt to understand her feelings.

It is impossible to understand another person's feelings if you do not understand your own. Therefore, men have to talk about and pay attention to their feelings to develop a point of reference for identifying with their partners' feelings. Once they establish this point of refer-ence, they need to learn how to listen actively and focus on their partners' emotional communications.

We have laid the groundwork for talking about men's feelings in previous chapters. Men need to accept the responsibility for changing the patterns, developing a language for feelings, becoming secure with themselves as men, and having the courage to overcome the limitations of traditional masculinity.

Empathy for a partner's emotional life means understanding feel-ings and thoughts that are different from one's own. Masculine social-ization discourages the development of this skill. Instead of cooperat-ing, which focuses on the needs of everyone, a man often learns to self-assert and compete, which focuses only on his needs. Fred was aware of his own thoughts and desires. His wife's needs were not only foreign to him, at times they felt like a threat. Fred's coping style was to re-emphasize and refocus on his own perspective, as if his experience were the only one that counted. At the same time, he desperately needed his wife's approval and acceptance. Fred's masculine needs for dominance and approval made the relationship unsatisfying for him and emotionally unsafe for his wife.

WHAT MASCULINE NEEDS MOST IMPAIR MEN'S RELATIONAL SKILLS?

Men experience a basic paradox that makes relational skills difficult to develop. They are often dependent on women, but at the same time they feel the need to dominate women. As we discussed in Chapter 2, dependency is rooted largely in early childhood psychological issues of anxious attachment. Men's domination of women can be seen as originating in the defense against this attachment anxiety and in the cultural demand for men to be powerful and to control women. In marriage, a man often finds himself uncomfortable with either being too emotionally close or too distant from his wife. He seeks validation from her when his dependency needs predominate; he seeks distance from her when his domination needs are highlighted. Although the dilemma of "not too close, not too far away" is difficult to resolve for both men and women, the prospect of attachment for women tends to not be as fraught with ambivalence as it is for men.

The need to dominate women means that men tend to pay attention to only their own needs and avoid developing the relational skills that might lead them to cooperate instead of compete. If, as we have previously stated, traditional masculinity is the effort to look like a man in the eyes of other men, then empathy for women threatens this kind of masculinity. This self-centered drive to dominate a relationship in order to feel safe is called *masculine narcissism*, which is rooted in many of the dynamics of masculine depression. The antidote to masculine narcissism is empathy.

WHAT IS NARCISSISM?

Narcissus is a character in Greek mythology who becomes so enthralled by his own reflection in a pond that he falls in love with himself. According to the myth, he cannot bring himself to look away, and so he remains transfixed, staring at his own reflection, until he dies. Thus, narcissism describes an extreme and destructive type of self-love, or, more accurately, a way of protecting oneself against the fear that one is defective and unlovable. Narcissists hide their low self-esteem by bragging about themselves and expecting others to admire them. Because they cannot face their vulnerable feelings, they have little empathy for themselves. They have not developed empathy for others because they lack a reference point for vulnerable feelings and because they focus all of their attention on themselves.

Narcissism is a defense against vulnerability, hiding insecurity behind arrogance and uncertainty behind bravado. The outward appearance is self-confident, effective, admirable, and independent. The inner reality—the pain behind the mask—is underconfident, incompetent, unlovable, and dependent. The extremely self-focused and distorted character of narcissism makes the person unable to have empathy for another person's needs, thoughts, and feelings. In this kind of one-way relationship, the partner is a *narcissistic extension*—someone who will hold up the metaphorical mirror so that the reflection can be admired. Talented, attractive, and/or wealthy narcissists have little difficulty finding people to do so (because, after all, they do have some admirable qualities), but even the most doting and devoted person grows weary of having his or her own needs neglected. One's arms can become very tired from constantly holding up a mirror.

Narcissism often leads a man to compulsively control his partner in an effort to make sure that his needs take priority, to blame his bad feelings on her because he cannot face them himself, to be unable to take care of his own emotional needs, and to continually avoid insight into his behavior. These behaviors force his partner to tiptoe around his temper, hide her own feelings, avoid giving him feedback on his negative behavior, and attend to his every emotional need as if he were a baby.

The root of the word narcissism is the Greek word *narke*, meaning "to deaden." It is also the root word for *narcotic*. Just as a drug abuser is addicted to a substance that deadens physical sensation and feeling, the narcissist is addicted to the self, and his feeling and sensation are also deadened. The narcissist becomes so absorbed in presenting a self-important image that his inner life becomes impoverished. He wants to be loved but cannot give love, and yet he compulsively seeks relationships because he is dependent on others for admiration.

How Is Narcissism Related to Masculine Depression and Lack of Empathy?

Depression results from the sense that one is a fundamentally flawed person and that nothing can be done about it. Internally, the narcissistic man experiences himself as worthless, but he tries to compensate for these feelings by orchestrating others to take care of him. If he has some admirable qualities, he may be successful in doing so in the short term, but nobody can possibly fulfill all of the unmet emotional needs inherent in traditional masculinity—to do so would require around-the-clock attention.

Men's narcissism is manifested in relationships. In the early stages of a relationship, the excitement of a new attraction tends to put individuals on their best behavior and allows them to ignore faults in the other person. The relationship tends to have an almost magical quality we call "infatuation." This extremely pleasurable state is more the result of falling in love with the *fantasy* of the other person rather than with the actual person. After a while, one has to give up the fantasy and deal with the reality of being in a relationship with a human being who is not always admiring, happy, emotionally available, or sexually exciting. Frequently, a man has difficulty accepting the reality that his partner cannot be perfect and meet all of his needs. When a little bit of the magic wears off, conflict tends to ensue, creating a difficult period of adjustment for even the healthiest individual. Men often find this stage depressing. Their hopes have been raised, only to be dashed.

After this loss of fantasized healing, the narcissistic man tends to devalue his partner and see her as less valuable than before. The partner becomes weary and angry about being exploited and thus becomes less willing to admire the man and subordinate her needs to his. Inevitably, he is struck with his own vulnerability and worthlessness, which is depressing. He is prone to temper tantrums, pouting, and aggression against the partner (for instance, by having affairs or denigrating her in public under the guise of good-natured teasing), which serves to further alienate her emotionally. When she becomes angry and less admiring of him, or she leaves him, he becomes despondent, as he does not have the psychological resources to care for himself emotionally.

Empathy is the opposite of narcissism. Empathy requires a person to focus on another person's feelings rather than just his or her own. The ability to do so rests critically on the person developing the emotional maturity to move beyond self-absorption. This process is difficult because of that central feature of masculine depression: dissociation from feelings. His emotional experiences are distorted by his defenses against vulnerability but he must reconnect with these feelings if he is to have any hope of identifying with someone else's feelings and constructing a healthy relationship. The narcissistic style is self-defeating and it feeds depression, as the following case illustrates:

Bobby's Story

Bobby is a versatile and talented man. He is a successful attorney at a large law firm. In his spare time, he excels in two interesting pursuits—stand-up comedy and full-contact karate. He is good enough at both of them to attain a semi-professional level of accomplishment—he spends an average of two weekends a month on the road performing comedy, and he has a prize fight about once every six weeks.

Bobby called me one evening in a state of panic. He said that he needed to see me right away and wanted to come to my house for an emergency session. After assessing his suicide potential, I determined that he would be okay meeting with me the following morning, when I had an available appointment time. He desperately pleaded with me to come in that evening, but eventually agreed to hold off until the next day.

Bobby arrived twenty minutes early for his appointment, hoping to get some extra time in case of a cancellation or a short session. He had been up all night. His face was red and puffy from crying, and he was collapsed in his chair when I went out to the waiting room to greet him.

Bobby had barely sat down in my office before he began to cry again. His live-in girlfriend of eighteen months had just left him again. He had returned from a comedy engagement to find a note from her stating that she no longer wanted to live with him. She had taken the opportunity of his absence to remove all of her belongings from the apartment.

Bobby felt that it was necessary to explain the entire history of the relationship to me, and he began to do so in exquisite detail and overdramatic fashion. He included specific dates of important events and spoke of these events in present tense: "January 5 last year: she leaves me after only three months together. I run to her best friend's house and stayed outside for four hours pleading with her to take me back. Three days later, she finally does. He described a volatile relationship with extreme highs and lows, marked with frequent breakups followed by intensely sexual and (pseudo-) intimate reconciliations. But he had the feeling that this time, it was final. She had taken steps to make sure he would not be able to find her. At the end of his story, he pleaded with me to help him understand, saying,"Why doesn't she love me? I'm a funny comedian, an excellent lawyer, and a damn good fighter."

This statement was the essence of Bobby's extreme depression and his distortion of healthy relationships. To him, being *loveable* meant being *admirable*, and he had no concept of giving to another person except by entertaining her or exciting her sexually. Now that she had left, he could not tolerate being alone with the terrible feelings that he could no longer defend. Because of his emotional emptiness, he needed someone else to constantly reassure him of his value. He tried to replace her with me, which is why he wanted a special crisis session the evening before, and also why he dropped out of treatment once he was able to resummon his narcissistic defenses. Although I told him in the session that I was concerned that he would drop out (since I knew that his tolerance for vulnerable feeling was so low) and made a strong recommendation that he resist this urge, he did not return. Because he could not stay with his discomfort, he could not learn how to deal with it.

What Is "Masculine Narcissism"?

As we have seen, many men compensate for relational weaknesses by hiding behind facades of invulnerability, specialness, and independence in order to feel emotionally safe. This strategy works only as long as the partner does not threaten the facade. Men frequently see their partners not as individuals with whom to relate, but as proof of their own abilities and attractiveness. *Masculine narcissism* is the inability to see one's partner as an individual, free to feel her own feelings, have her own desires, and make her own decisions. His need to appear masculine denies her need to be a treated like a human being. He lacks empathy for her as he focuses solely on his image as a man. His overattention to this image makes it difficult for either of them to be fully human.

Men experience the conflicts of both needing and fearing attachment and intimacy. "Not too close, not too far away" is the "rule" that results from this conflict. As long as she abides by this rule by subordinating her needs to his, the relationship is stable, although it may not be satisfying. When she breaks the rule and takes control of herself, she gains appropriate power in the relationship. He fears that this means she will leave him or that he will be emasculated by losing control and mastery. By "becoming her own person," i.e., gaining control over her own feelings, decisions, behaviors, desires, etc., she becomes a threat to him. Her ability to reject him threatens him because of the fears that he unconsciously harbors about himself.

Doug: Masculine Narcissism

Doug's marriage was threatened by his masculine narcissism. He was successful by all social appearances. He knew how to effectively sell his products to clients by manipulating them into saying "yes" to his ideas. He was handsome, athletic, financially successful, and a rising star in his business. Recently his wife had left him. She had been "sold" too many things: the need for his various expensive toys, frequent pressure for sex, risky financial investments, and frequent social contact with business partners whom she did not like. Doug was stunned. He kept saying, "She should feel . . . ," "She should know that . . . ," "Doesn't she see that I love her?" Doug did not know his wife. He had relied on her as a narcissistic extension of himself, feeding him images of his success, importance, power, and intelligence. He was so clouded by his own needs and desires that his wife's needs never occurred to him. When the crisis came, he tried to use logic to rationalize the problem away and develop a "yes set" in her that would bring her back into the emotional and perceptual world in which he lived, but she did not return. The more his arguing and pressuring failed, the more he argued and pressured. She simply said

"I don't love you anymore." He continued, "You should feel good about our lives; you should know I love you; you should know I can't live without you; you should want to have this marriage." Doug expressed only his own thoughts and feelings. Like an egocentric child, he could not see that his wife is and always has been a separate person.

As Doug's therapist, I tried several approaches to help him develop empathy for his wife. All failed. So I turned the tables on Doug and told him, "I know this person who loves you, knows from the bottom of this person's heart that you two would make a perfect couple. This person absolutely knows that once you two meet, you'll be forever in love. The person's name is Jim." Doug was not especially homophobic, but he was not homosexual either. He would be unmoved by a man having strong desires for him. Because I presented these feelings as coming from a man's point of view, Doug was able to accept that they could be different from his own. He had not accepted his wife's different feelings because he perceived her as an extension of himself and, because she is a woman, he considered her less than a whole person.

Doug began to understand what it was like for his wife to have her own feelings in spite of his efforts to make her feel what he wanted her to feel. In fact, he understood that her feelings are not created or influenced by his desires, no matter how persuasively he argues. He began to look at the effect that his "salesmanship" had on her in other areas as well. Once Doug could develop empathy for his wife, he could understand that her feelings did not have to match his needs. He had needed her to accept his resolution of the conflict and not feel angry. She needed to feel angry because he was still not accepting her feelings. Once he developed empathy for her feelings, he no longer had to run over her in order to resolve conflicts. Empathy broke the pattern of masculine narcissism and made it possible to begin the process of rebuilding the relationship.

* * *

It is entirely possible to be masculine and to be in an intimate relationship at the same time. Both Fred and Doug eventually found this to be true. Both remained successful, athletic, and competitive in the proper contexts. By facing their fears in relationships with women, both men overcame the limitations that these fears bring, and both found that women can enhance and not threaten men.

The ending to Bobby's story is not as happy. Because his extreme narcissism created such a self-absorbed and emotionally needy state, the anxiety of having nobody to soothe and admire him left him in a state of panic, which rendered him unable to learn any of the skills necessary to participate in a healthy relationship. It is very likely that, once he was able to muster his emotional defenses, he would fall back on the only strategy that he knows for dealing with his needs and his pain—seducing somebody else into admiring him. If he were successful in doing so, he would feel safer and happier for a short while, but his psychological deficits would dictate that the cycle of depression, narcissism, and relationship conflict would be destined to play itself out again and again.

WHY DO MEN LACK EMPATHY FOR WOMEN IN INTIMATE RELATIONSHIPS?

Traditional masculinity denies women their personhood and robs men of empathic living. In Chapter 6, we examined how masculinity might be seen primarily as a relationship among men. In traditionally gendered heterosexual relationships, women help men to maintain their masculine appearance with other men by being beautiful, subservient, and dependent. Men do not often look beyond their own fears and need for control to see the strain that traditional masculinity places on women. Doug could not empathize with his wife's feelings because he unconsciously saw her as less than a person, i.e., a woman. When I presented her as "him," he could acknowledge that she could have feelings that were different than his. Doug may not have understood the full social meaning of my intervention. Traditional masculinity allows men to only see other men as independent persons who deserve to be taken seriously. Women are not accorded this status. It was easier for Doug to empathize with a "him" than with his wife.

Men's inability to empathize with women has numerous roots. We have described the process by which masculinity becomes defined as antifemininity. Through this process, men learn to devalue the feminine and, by extension, women. A long history of cultural patterns have allowed and even encouraged men to control women and regard them as objects, second-class citizens, and nonpersons. For instance, women have been expected to submerge their individual identities to men by taking their husband's surnames at marriage and even referring to themselves using their husband's first names ("Mrs. John Smith").

Males are indoctrinated into antifeminine beliefs and fears early, often, and pervasively in their lives. The more that women are considered to be psychologically different and deficient compared to men, the more that men are discouraged from empathizing with women. Doug and Bobby may not have understood these influences on their lives, but they lived them nevertheless.

HOW DOES ONE OVERCOME MASCULINE NARCISSISM?

If romantic relationships were a coin, affection and love would be one side; anger and conflict would be the other. Everyone can accept that there is no coin with only one side, and the same is true of relationships. Anger is a natural part of relationships, and ultimately the appropriate expression of anger is also both an expression of trust (I care and trust enough to let you know what is really important to me) and an effort to improve the relationship (If you can understand why this bothers me and help me to change it, we can be much closer, so I will tell you when I am angry). Many men tend to interpret anger in a relationship as a sign of masculine failure ("I'm not being a successful and fully competent man") and a threat (her anger undermines his sense of masculine dominance and unconsciously reminds him of mother's anger and the potential for isolation in early development). These patterns may have understandable origins in development. They bring heartache and loss in adulthood. Part of overcoming these patterns involves cognitive changes on the part of men, i.e., changing the way men think about relationships and about themselves. For instance, purposefully reminding yourself that her anger is not a threat can lead to an opportunity for growth and intimacy. Part of overcoming these patterns is reminding yourself that you are still a man even though you are not in control of every moment.

One very important healing process for men is to acknowledge the powerful fantasies of unlimited success, power, and brilliance. As we stated before, boys tend to identify with larger-than-life images of successful men. Unconsciously, they feel inadequate when they compare themselves to these images, and narcissism is a defense against the feelings of shame that accompany the unfavorable comparison of the real-life self with the larger than life icon. When men live in a world of narcissistic fantasy, they are psychologically incapable of entering a truly reciprocal relationship with another person. These fantasies have the quality of an addictive drug—they are highly pleasurable, intoxicating, and they distract the man from the less attractive aspects of life. At the same time, the potential for harm from these fantasies is considerable.

Gaining insight into narcissistic processes can be very helpful in the quest to reduce the destructive power of unrealistic fantasy. Men need to acknowledge their deep wishes to be strikingly attractive, incredibly athletic, profoundly intelligent, and overwhelmingly charming. It is important to learn to talk with other people about these fantasies and to develop a sense a humor about how ridiculous they are. Doing so reduces the level of shame that accompanies the fantasy. It makes the unconscious conscious and therefore less powerful. It frees the man to truly appreciate his gifts and talents, rather than to see himself as flawed because he is human.

Men can also work on healing narcissism within their relationships. Following are three simple and straightforward methods for overcoming the relational problems faced by Doug, Fred, Bobby, and many men.

1. *Learn to listen to what she says, not to what you think she should say, think, or feel.* As Fred learned, what she feels and what he thinks she should feel are not necessarily the same. Relationships are hindered until her feelings are meaningfully understood. When men react to what they think she should say, think, or feel, their judgments are most often inaccurate. Men end up reacting to their own fears of what she feels and their own defenses against these fears, a process known as projection. There is no place for "the real her" in the midst of all these projected and distorted masculine fears.

2. *Separate her feelings from your fears and get in touch with your own fears.* Men frequently fear women's independence and individuality. Controlling her feelings and behavior has been a

way of controlling the fears that men harbor about themselves but have not been able to name. Her feelings do not mean that you are less of a man or that you are not fully in control; they only reflect important experiences for her. Acknowledging one's own fears allows one to change the idea that, "There's something wrong with her; I have to fight for my own power" into "Conflict is a natural part of a relationship; I want to join her to help us resolve it."

3. *Find key phrases that assist you in talking to yourself in helpful ways.* People do not do their best thinking or problem solving when they are in intense emotional conflicts. Men can find simple phrases to say to themselves that can pull them out of the reflexive need to defend and attack. Phrases such as, "I can work this through without yelling," "Loving her for life is more important than winning this argument," or "I may not understand right now, but I love her enough to try to understand better" can help recenter a man when the adrenalin starts pumping and clear thinking stops.

WHAT STEPS CAN MEN TAKE TO ACQUIRE SKILLS FOR SUCCESSFUL RELATIONSHIPS?

Men who want to work on becoming more skilled in a relationship would do well to develop the following attributes:

1. *Commitment.* To use a parallel from traditional masculinity, any athlete knows that training is difficult. Perseverance through the hard times is a necessary part of "getting better." Failures point to the areas, skills, and muscles that need more work. A couple cannot work on their relationship unless they are committed to staying together and dealing with their problems.

    For men, this issue is often directly related to masculine depression. Working through the "not too close, not too far away" issue requires a commitment to learn from mistakes, tolerate the anxiety, and develop new skills. Maintaining the "not too close, not too far away" issue, on the other hand, requires doing what men usually do.

The first step in repairing and enhancing a relationship is commitment, and no magic formula exists for it. The man has to decide whether or not he is willing to commit the time, effort, and emotional risk necessary to improve his marriage. Learning to behave differently is a matter of *skill*. Committing oneself to new learning is a matter of *will.*

This kind of work is usually more difficult for men, who often have to learn to talk about gender, feelings, and relationships. Women usually have a lifetime of experience in this kind of talking, as it is part of feminine culture. Therefore, in committing to undertake a course of change, men are committing to learning a set of rather difficult skills. The payoff is that these skills will help the man to develop more satisfying relationships of all kinds and to feel more comfortable with himself wherever he goes.

2. *Taking off your gender glasses.* Psychologist Sandra Bem describes some people as looking "through the lenses of gender."[1] In other words, they tend to see the world in "masculine" and "feminine" categories. American culture encourages men to see women as people whose value is less than equal to that of men. Centuries of patriarchy have resulted in men's dominance of women throughout the world. This gender arrangement gets in the way of healthy intimacy, which is based on equal power in both partners. The view of women as underlings feeds masculine narcissism and inhibits empathy, as it encourages men to expect women to subordinate their needs to those of men.

We have described how masculine socialization dehumanizes men by stripping them of their emotional lives and making their relationships less than satisfying. Men can begin to free themselves from the unhealthy and unnecessary constraints of masculinity by learning about gender pressures on their own lives and on the lives of women.

3. *Empathy for the self.* A man must be able to access his emotional life to understand that of his partner. Follow the suggestions for developing empathy for the self in Chapter 5.

4. *Empathy with your partner.* We have focused this entire chapter on the development of empathy with one's partner. Following are some structured and specific techniques for doing so—listening, imagining, and connecting.

Listening sounds easy, but it really isn't. It involves a full effort to hear and understand the other person. It is an active process in which one works hard to really experience what the other person is experiencing. Some couples develop listening skills by using an exercise in which one partner makes a statement, and then the other partner must restate (in different words) what the person has said before going on with the conversation. Men are often at a lower level of skill development than many women in this area, as they have been trained to use conversations for self-assertion and to use listening for task (rather than emotional) reasons.

Imagining is putting oneself in the other person's place and trying to experience the world as that person does. You can start to answer questions such as: "How does my partner see the world?"; "What are his/her most cherished values?"; "What kind of things really get under his/her skin?"; and "How does he/she experience me?"

Connecting involves building bridges between your emotional experiences and those of your partner. Once you have a good idea of how your partner experiences the world, you can try to think of events in your own life that produce similar emotional reactions. One man recalls a powerful instance of connecting:

> My wife had been telling me how fearful she was of talking with her mother, who always seems to tell her how inadequate and immoral she is. I tried to be supportive, but I just couldn't really understand it. I thought I had no experience to connect it with—I mean, my mother is a real sweetheart. Then, one night I had a really bad nightmare—someone was chasing me and trying to kill me. I woke up feeling incredibly fearful and vulnerable. Later, it occurred to me that this was the same kind of feeling my wife must have when she thinks about her mother's power to shame her so badly.

We have all felt the basic human emotions of fear, sadness, joy, grief, and anger. Connecting one's own experience to that of one's partner creates an emotional bond that can form the basis of the relationship. It is where empathy for the self meets empathy for the partner.

People in healthy relationships have made the skills of listening, imagining, and connecting into habits. As with any skills, they become better and more natural with practice. Often people discount their abilities to learn these skills because they do not come naturally at first. They tend to say, "I can't do that; I guess it's just not me." But remember the first time you tried anything that was fairly complex? For example, hitting a golf ball, typing, playing a musical instrument, driving a standard transmission, or performing a job skill? Chances are that these were awkward too, and you weren't very good at them, but, over time, you developed some competence. These interpersonal skills are no different.

5. *Working on the relationship with your partner.* Once a couple learns to understand the gender and personal issues that have affected the relationship, as well as each partner's emotional experiences, they are ready to transform their relationship from one that emphasizes competition to one that stresses cooperation. They begin to see their marriage as a joint project in which each person contributes and benefits. They begin to see disputes as mutual problems to be solved rather than conflicts in which one person wins and the other loses.

Forming the habits and attitudes we have described above is most of the battle. Partners who understand and trust each other will have few difficulties of an interpersonal nature. Still, conflicts emerge in any relationship, and it is helpful to learn specific skills to manage them. One simple formula involves four steps: *griping, narrowing, formulating,* and *collaborating.*

You probably don't need a definition of *griping.* It is simply complaining about what one does not like, and people do it naturally when they feel dissatisfied. It has a purpose—it gets issues out in the open and communicates feelings about the way things are going. Griping only becomes negative under two circumstances. The first is when griping involves character attacks and extremely hurtful statements, such as, "You were a complete idiot when you . ." or "I hate you when you . . ." Partners need to keep in mind that, even though they are griping, they are talking to a person whom they love and with whom they want to connect. It is also important to own your own reactions. "I get upset when . . ." is different from "You make me angry when . . ."

The other scenario in which griping becomes negative is all too common. It is the case in which griping becomes the sole form of conflict resolution. If griping is all you do, the conversation turns into a competition in which each person attempts to show the other person that he/she has the better gripes. No productive work is possible if the couple stops at griping.

Narrowing involves taking the most serious gripe and focusing on it. After a while, you should be asking your partner, "Of all the things you mentioned, which one bothers you the most?" Often, if the most serious gripe is addressed, the others can be tolerated. A wife might say, "I really get angry when you ignore me when you're talking to your male friends." She may have also griped about not being consulted when her husband makes social plans, but the lack of social attention is foremost in her reaction.

Formulating is transforming a gripe into a problem to be agreed upon and then solved by the couple. In the above scenario, the couple agrees that there are ways in which both partners can behave differently in order to alleviate the wife's discomfort in these situations.

When a couple can share a formulation of a problem, they can collaborate to find solutions and agree upon those solutions. In the above example, many solutions are possible: he could make attempts to include her in conversations; she could feel free to participate in other activities besides the conversation; he could make conscious efforts to shorten the conversations or engage in the activities less frequently; they could make efforts to cultivate social relationships with other couples and women.

Now that the couple has generated a list of possible solutions, they are ready to *negotiate*. Clearly, some possible solutions can be unworkable. In the above scenario, the wife's staying home or doing some other social activity would be an acceptable alternative for some couples but not for others. Partners need to compromise and use their creativity to find solutions that they can live with and commit to.

HOW DO YOU RECOGNIZE
A POWER STRUGGLE?

Power struggles are characterized by the effort to win rather than to solve a problem. They create resentful and distrustful feelings in partners and damage the relationship. The central feature of masculine narcissism is an exclusive focus on the self, which causes the partner to feel as if she is not being heard or considered. It is the experience of being overpowered, and the natural response is to struggle to regain power. As a result, couples engage in a competition for power because neither trusts that the other one will share it. Men can improve the quality of their relationships by learning to recognize when he is involved in a power struggle and take steps to "fight fairly," i.e., resolve differences through cooperative efforts. The following behaviors are signs of a power struggle:

1. *You stop listening to your partner.* While she is speaking, you use that time to plan what you are going to say next.
2. *You rehearse an argument.* You anticipate conflict, and so you plan how you are going to verbally attack your partner. You try to guess what kind of strategy she will employ in defense, and you plan a counterattack.
3. *You feel the physical sensations of conflict.* Your heart races and you feel the "adrenaline rush" that accompanies threat.
4. *You "throw in the kitchen sink."* You bring up past transgressions by your partner in order to seek the moral high ground.
5. *Winning becomes more important than feeling better.* Your partner becomes your adversary. You lose sight of the fact that you love this person and have chosen to spend your life with her.

When normal occasional relationship conflicts become power struggles, couples frequently resort to "dirty fighting"—attack, counterattack, and character assassination. This style of dealing with conflict is counterproductive to the goal of living together cooperatively and intimately. Since conflict is inevitable, couples must learn how to fight fairly when it occurs.

HOW DO YOU FIGHT FAIRLY
WITHOUT ABUSE OR CAPITULATION?

Fighting fairly means avoiding the abuse of power. It means overcoming the urge to yell, hit, or threaten. It means not competing to win, but rather cooperating so that both of you may win. Many of the initial defensive reactions for men involve fear and anger accompanied by an adrenalin rush. Behaviors that flow from such highly charged emotional states tend to be impulsive, defensive, and sometimes dangerous. At times, the first step in fighting fairly is to take a time out to stop this rush in order to begin to think in calmer and more helpful ways. Here is a simple time-out technique that men can use to begin to control their behavior and use the other skills we have been discussing.

Time Out

In order to change, you have to do something different. As simple as this statement sounds, couples frequently forget it and wait for someone else to do the changing. Hence, they remain stuck in the power struggle process of attack and counterattack. Properly executed, a time-out procedure is brief, structured, specific, and effective. Each partner has a task to do and trusts the other to do his/her part. There are three simple and effective steps:

1. When couples are "getting into it again" it can be helpful to physically separate from each other for a short period of time. This time can be as brief as ninety seconds or as long as five minutes, but under nonabusive situations should rarely go any longer. The initial separation prevents the old pattern from continuing and prepares each to actually do something different. If, at the end of the time out, they start the old pattern again they can easily begin the time out again, until they get it right.
2. The second step is based on the principle that you cannot simultaneously be tense and relaxed, and that change safely occurs when an individual is physically relaxed. While separated, each person relaxes his/her body, starting with breathing and quickly extending to major muscle groups. We all have

characteristic ways in which our bodies deal with tension. Some people get a tight sensation in their stomachs, others get tight shoulders or necks, others shake. During this step, each person regulates his/her breathing back to normal and relaxes.

3. The third step involves self-talk, one of the best tools adults have at their disposal to facilitate change and calm themselves through difficult times. Rather than using the time out to rehearse the upcoming argument, people can say exactly what is important to help them be in charge of themselves: "I can calm down and get my point across without yelling." "He/She is more important to me than losing my temper." "I can do this without yelling like my father did; I'm different from him in this way." "I can be the kind of man I've always wanted to be, not the screamer I've become."

When both partners are ready, and not before, they can come back together and either try again or use one of the other techniques listed here. The point of the time-out technique is to give couples a brief but punctuated experience of doing something different. It gives men a way to resist the pull of traditional masculine development and build appropriate communication patterns instead. Men can quickly learn not to use anger and temper when such reactions run counter to the goal of handling conflict in a relationship-enhancing way.

HOW CAN MEN LEARN TO BE MATES AND NOT MASTERS?

Mates are cherished equals. Mates never try to hurt, mistreat, or take advantage of each other. Couples must learn to develop trust and safety in order to have a cooperative relationship. The following technique can be helpful in transforming the competitive relationship into a cooperative one.

"I Was Wrong": Breaking the Cultural Binds

Our culture honors being right and winning. The irony is that to grow we have to see and admit our mistakes, not just talk about how we are right. In problem marriages, each partner ignores his/her own errors but gets angry at the other for doing the same. The result is a power struggle. In order for growth to occur, each person needs to admit his/her mistakes, but neither does for fear of "losing."

An old saying states that marriage is the act of revealing. The more partners reveal themselves to each other, the deeper and stronger the marriage becomes. This technique has each person do what is most difficult: talk only about his/her own mistakes, and say nothing about the other's. Both partners need to agree to collaborate using this technique. Coming to this can be extremely difficult, and frequently couples need a mediator or therapist to help get it started.

In this technique, following the rules is very important. One person begins by saying "I was wrong to . . ." and admits one thing that he/she did to contribute to the problem they are currently experiencing as a couple. Statements are brief and do not reference the other person. Statements such as "I was wrong to think you are a good person" are not what this technique is about. Once the first person has made a statement, the other person makes one. Then the really difficult part begins: they go back and forth two more times. The first time is easy; the second and third time require more soul searching and revealing of self to the other. Neither person can comment about what the other person said in any negative way, and they do not comment at all until the entire technique is completed. Once they have completed this task, they can resume the original "argument." When applied consistently, this way of changing patterns results in personal growth and greatly enhanced marital trust and safety.

An example of a complete dialogue is as follows:

Person 1: I was wrong to slam the door when I came in.

Person 2: I was wrong to yell right away.

Person 1: I was wrong not to tell you I was angry about being late.

Person 2: I was wrong to wait until the last minute to get ready.

Person 1: I was wrong to leave all the planning and preparations up to you.

Person 2: I was wrong for trying to do it all and getting resentful instead of asking for help.

Think how different this "discussion" would be if it went like this:

Person 1: Stop yelling!

Person 2: Well, you slammed the door!

Person 1: You always wait until the last minute!

Person 2: You're always angry!

Person 1: *You're* always angry!

Person 2: You never help!

WHAT IS THE BEST WAY TO TALK?

We have presented a way of looking at men's development that suggests there are several ghosts that haunt men's relationships. In Chapter 2 we described complexities in the mother-son relationship, and in Chapter 3 we described the origins of the locker room chorus. Both of these remain with men, in subtle form, like a ghost of earlier conflicts. These ghosts complicate relationships for men. Here is a way to talk that addresses reality and not history.

Face to Face: Chasing Away the Ghosts

Men and women frequently fail to understand each other. Their differences are rooted in the differential development discussed in Chapter 2 and the intense socialization process that we discussed in Chapter 3. Masculine identity is based on different assumptions, experiences, and dilemmas than feminine identity. Interaction between partners can be strongly influenced by the expectations each person brings to the relationship. Each partner uses these distorted expectations to predict what the other person thinks and feels. Most of these predictions are inaccurate and lead to blaming, arguing, and misunderstandings.

When couples break this pattern by sitting down and really looking at each other they can see what is present and what their mental representations prevent them from seeing. The best way for couples to talk and create a different experience for themselves is to sit with each other in a way that represents their marriage. If couples were to sit facing each other, knees touching knees, holding hands, and maintaining eye contact, they would be sculpting the vessel or the container that represents their marriage. This is the sitting arrangement in which each could actually see and meaningfully converse with the other. Under these conditions each could see who his/her spouse really is, not how he/she is represented in thought. People generally avoid this arrangement because it is very intense and revealing. But marriages endure best when there are opportunities to reveal and be seen in a safe manner. Men can see women as intimate partners, not threatening and alien individuals.

The sexism, self-focus, and emotional restrictedness of traditional masculinity make for frequent difficulties in heterosexual relationships. Men often find themselves stuck in the unhealthy relationship patterns of avoiding and dominating. Those who are able to address the roots of masculine depression and develop empathy for their partners can develop trusting, open, and satisfying relationships that move out of power struggles and into cooperation.

WHAT ARE THE ABCs OF CHANGE?

Affect
   —develop empathy

Behavior
   —calm yourself physically
   —do the self-talk
   —begin with "I was wrong"

Cognition
   —find a key phrase to remind yourself of what you want to do

Chapter 8

Relations with Family

I wondered about my neighbor's struggles with masculinity one morning. I found his three-year-old son crying on the porch. It was about nine o'clock on a particularly cold October morning and I was walking past his house. There, curled up at the base of the front porch door was a little boy in his pajamas without shoes or socks, pounding on the (locked) front door. He was screaming, "DADDY! DADDY!" When he saw me he cried, "I want my daddy." I walked up to him and attempted to calm him. Then I knocked on the door until his father arrived five minutes later. He had just stepped out of the shower, quickly sized up the situation, and said, "I thought the house was too quiet—Billy, don't go outside like this again." That was it. He turned to me and made some comment about kids being unpredictable and then changed the conversation to the work he was getting ready to do. I reacted with surprise at his response. Had this happened to my child, I hope that I would have sensed his distress, picked him up and held him tightly until we both stopped crying, and asked him to tell me what he thought and felt.

I do not know whether my being male made my neighbor show less empathy for his son or whether this was his usual behavior. Whatever the cause, in that moment the father did not identify with his son's pain. Consequently, he did not comfort his son. The father was in his own world, taking a shower and getting ready for work. He had lost awareness that his son was in the house and required his attention and guidance. As a result, the boy was locked out of father's world, literally and figuratively.

That day, the son learned something from his father about the importance of feelings and about what he can expect from others when he is frightened and in need. He learned something about how attentive fathers are to the needs of others, at least when they are in the home. He also watched his father act like a stereotypical man in the presence of another man, refusing to show feelings, admit weakness, or own up to his mistakes.

Mikey: Aggressive at School

Six-year-old Mikey was referred for counseling because he was aggressive at school, didn't finish his work, and frequently yelled at the teacher. He was repeating kindergarten and it looked as if Mikey might repeat the grade again next year unless his behavior and concentration improved. The teacher suggested that the parents seek counseling and/or medication to help Mikey. Mikey's mother made the initial contact with the counseling agency. As requested by the therapist, both parents attended the first session without Mikey.

A man's first opportunity to meet and talk with a therapist often happens in this way. He comes in to "help out" when either his partner or his children have symptoms. Sometime during these family sessions, Dad gets the opportunity to tell *his* story. The specifics may change but the theme is the same—Dad has a problem with his temper. He had been physically abusive to his wife in the past, and his son had witnessed it. Although Dad doesn't hit family members or throw things anymore, he still yells. To his son, it seems as if he yells all of the time. When asked what he is angry about, Dad vaguely answers that he has always been this way. His family does not like him because he has "an attitude." When asked about his family of origin, he readily discloses that he was the one who always got the beatings, and that he is a much better father to Mikey than his father was to him. He even goes on to say that as far as he is concerned, he has broken the chain of abuse. He seems to be wanting credit for merely refraining from striking his wife or children.

This hard-working man is sincere in his belief that he is giving Mikey a better father-son relationship and a better family life than he had received, and, in a way, he is right. But, although he may have stopped the chain of physical abuse, there is still a lot of emotional pain in this family. And it is the kind of pain that doesn't get comforted because this man has learned to mask his own emotional suffering. The boy's thinly disguised hurt is clearly expressed in his aggressive behavior. Behind this behavior lies a confused, frightened, and angry boy. If we look only at his behaviors, i.e., his appearance, we miss the pain that he is learning to disguise with his aggression and distractibility.

During this first session, Dad comments on how the ten-month-old baby girl cries when he yells. He observes, "She's sensitive." When asked, "Who else in the family is sensitive?" Mom volunteers that Mikey is sensitive. His feelings are hurt easily. Not surprisingly, when we reviewed the pattern of Mikey's outbursts, many could be traced to these hurt feelings. When asked, "Who else in the family might be sensitive?" Mom volunteers that she is, and that she handles her emotional pain by withdrawing from others. With only one family member left unmentioned, when asked, "Who else might be sensitive?" Mom confidently says, "That's it." There are a few seconds of silence, and Dad smirks. He turns to her and offers, "This counselor thinks I'm sensitive." His wife gives testimony that he isn't sensitive at all. But he continues to smirk. The woman who had been married to him for eight years looks shocked. He never gave any clues to his sensitivity. She had only seen his aggressive and violent defenses, and she had good reasons not to look beyond those. His appearance was deceiving, even to his wife. He had hidden his sensitivity from her behind the mask of traditional masculinity. Maybe he thought that revealing his sensitivity would make him less of a "real man."

Of course Dad is sensitive. Anyone who is alive and human has feelings that can be hurt. The turning point of this first session occurred when Dad and Mom made the connection between the way that Mikey had learned to cover up his sadness and hurt with temper tantrums and other unregulated aggression, and the way that his Dad operates. Without expressions of these "sensitive feelings," Mikey and Dad had no way to learn to handle them except by acting out. Whether Dad or Mikey changes this pattern depends in large part on how Dad addresses his own sensitivity and his empathy for others, or more specifically, his parenting skills.

*   *   *

We began Chapter 2 with a gendered view of family structure. Relative to the emotional life and connectedness of a family, fathers are isolated too often. A boy sees a distant, mysterious, seemingly self-sufficient father and, without intending to do so, becomes that same father when he marries and has children. Masculine depression is quietly and subtly passed from father to son as a pattern of masculine behaviors, expectations, and experiences that are sustained in part by family interactions.

This pattern is understandable because of the way in which the unconscious mind works. In Chapter 4 we discussed how the masculine unconscious mind associates being in a primary relationship involving the female in the house with the dilemma, "not too close, not too far away." Time, place, and individual differences are not the language or the interest of the unconscious mind. Associations are. *Seeing* a father and *being* a father are similarly connected. As pattern-seeking organisms, we unconsciously develop a template, an unspoken and unrecognized set of expectations, that helps us understand how to behave and what to expect. We carry this template with us into future interactions. Mikey's dad has a template that describes a father in a family. Even when his conscious mind stopped his physically violent behavior, he continued to rely on the original template. Therefore, he persisted in a pattern of anger, emotional violence, distance, and fear of his "sensitivity." His interactive style reflected all that he had learned about being a man, a husband, and a father. This learned behavior prevented him from becoming the father that he desperately wanted to be.

Mikey's father and his father's father followed their own templates. We do not seek to imply that any of these men are not responsible for the damage they cause in their families. Nor do we seek to pathologize them and say that they are no better than their behaviors. We seek to hold them accountable for their behaviors and responsible for change, and a major tool for this change is insight into the processes by which the negative behavior and sense of self is produced. In this chapter we will present a model of healthy masculinity in a family. Our solution is neither easy nor simple. It is, however, needed and possible.

Distant, aloof fathers tend to beget distant, aloof fathers. Socialization adds to this process by solidifying traditional masculine standards of behavior. Males are punished for any behavior that, by masculine standards, is considered to be feminine. These behaviors include open displays of caring, allowing people to be more important than tasks, and being a cooperative part of a whole family. Many men enter family life primed for emotional isolation. After all, the home is socially defined as a woman's world. Traditional masculinity utilizes antifeminine attitudes to guide men into seemingly safe masculine behaviors. As we have discussed, traditional masculinity impairs relational skills, which are viewed as feminine and therefore regarded as dangerous. But families *are* relationships. Men need these relationships and intimate connections with partners and families, and their children and wives need the same with them.

Men face the same competing needs that they have experienced since their first introduction into traditional masculinity—the need to be fully human versus the need to appear masculine. Despite the fears that traditional masculinity imposes, over 90 percent of men marry at some point in their lives because they crave intimacy. Men need and seek intimate relationships as friends, husbands, and fathers. It is not the *desire* for relationships that is underdeveloped in men, it is the relational *skills* needed to fulfill this desire. Healthy family functioning requires such skills. Men have the abilities and desire to be good fathers. They need new experiences to develop new skills.

WHAT HAPPENS TO FATHERS IN PROBLEMATIC FAMILIES?

Couples and families tend to fall into a pattern in which mothers take all of the responsibility for the health, comfort, appearance, and happiness of the family. While they are doing the important domestic chores, fathers hit the "Dad Zone." Mothers probably call it "the dead zone," but it is the same zone that Dad saw his own father occupy. It is a place where he dissociates from family needs, patterns, and behaviors, leaving Mother to pick up the slack. He is in the "Dad Zone" because he feels out of his masculine element in the feminine world of the home. In the social model of masculinity, he feels the need to be protected from all that is feminine. Social and emotional family tasks have been mislabeled as "women's work"—places where femininity is needed to solve the problems of living. Even when Father is not at work, not with the guys, and not comfortable or knowledgeable about his children's needs, he still feels the need to be "not feminine." So he enters the "Dad Zone," a place of protection from the threats of the feminine, a place where masculinity translates into male privilege, where the newspaper or the TV are his domain, and where he responds in an automatic manner to notices such as "dinner's ready."

He observed the "Dad Zone" when he was a boy. His father appeared to live in it quite naturally. After all, Dad was there most of the time and no one ever said anything about it. Therefore, he assumes that the "Dad Zone" is the only place for a father to be when he is at home. In his experience, he never saw his father walk around the house knowing that he was supposed to be doing something but not knowing what that something was. He never saw his father feeling awkward trying to comfort the children and, in frustration, turning the task over to Mother. He never felt his father's sense of being useless or the fear that he was not really needed in the family. Instead he saw the "Dad Zone," that protective cloak from threats of femininity and uselessness. He did not understand that it is the "Dad Zone" that keeps mothers in the "Mom Zone," i.e., the place where mothers attend to all of the little things that keep a family moving through the week. Mothers fill the emotional needs of families, become the communication hubs, and carry on many parenting tasks because fathers get lost in the "Dad Zone." Children quickly learn whom to turn to for emotional and nurturing needs. Fathers see children's turning to their mothers as more evidence of their own domestic and emotional incompetence.

HOW DO YOU BECOME THE FATHER THAT YOU DID NOT HAVE?

The answer is deceptively simple—through the behaviors that your father did not do. Consider the following list of activities in a family:

- distinguishing between behavioral outbursts that are produced by fatigue as opposed to those produced by hurt feelings
- developing ways for children to overcome their fear of going to sleep and having nightmares
- listening when children are upset
- attending parent-teacher conferences
- chaperoning school field trips
- shopping for school clothes

- chauffeuring the children
- understanding that when the younger kids say they want the purple sweatshirt, they are actually referring to the one that is sea green
- negotiating the kids' wardrobes to balance useful clothing with current social fashions
- dealing with peer pressure constructively and empathically
- planning the week's meals and making sure that all of the needed ingredients are purchased *beforehand*
- doing laundry while helping with homework
- mopping the floor during the only available time when no one will be walking on it
- refilling soap and shampoo containers *before* they are empty
- scheduling and going to doctor and dentist visits
- wiping the toddlers after their first attempts at independence in the bathroom
- arranging for after-school playmates
- calling to schedule enrollment at day care centers before they are filled
- planning ahead for children's school vacation schedules during the summer
- arranging co-ops with other parents to provide coverage for children eight hours a day and five days a week
- reminding children to practice their musical instruments
- writing the personal notes on holiday cards to relatives
- participating in children's religious studies and spiritual development
- handling the social problems of popularity and rejection at school and with peers
- planning birthday parties and buying age-appropriate gifts
- sending special treats and personal notes in school lunches
- buying and sending birthday cards to grandparents and other family members
- remembering what breakfast foods the children will eat when they are in a hurry
- preparing younger children for social events by telling them how to behave and respond

- making sure fruits and vegetables are served and eaten
- avoiding the need to rely too much on fast food
- keeping up with snack times and kids' nutritional needs
- planning for children's needs during long car trips
- knowing where the winter and summer clothes are and transitioning them through the kids' dresser drawers as needed
- buying presents for the children's friends when they are invited to birthday parties
- sending thank you notes for gifts received

None of these activities require breast milk. Yet in most families they are performed almost exclusively by the mother. These are the tasks that build emotional connectedness. A man has to be emotionally invested and connected enough in the family to pay attention to all these details. It is impossible to fully, and as an equal partner, participate in these activities and at the same time maintain the dissociation from feelings, self, and the needs of others that embody the traps of masculine depression. Men who perform these tasks become as emotionally connected to families as mothers are. Their masculinity is enhanced and enriched. Their emotional life is more full and expressed. Their relationships are mutual and cooperative. And these men have lost none of the skills needed to work, compete when necessary, and provide safety for their families.

The long list above is by no means inclusive. As most mothers know, it can never be. In fact, mothers usually know just how incomplete it actually is. The daily demands of family living are more than we could begin to list here. Moreover, the needs of families evolve. Indeed, recognizing and keeping up with the changing needs and patterns of family activities is, in itself, part of attending to the family's needs. A parent cannot track the changing needs of the family unless he or she is fully engaged in the family's daily life.

These activities are vital in every family. We could say that these activities *are* the family. They are the family energy, and the way in which they are performed characterizes the uniqueness of each and every family. When they are somehow quietly assigned to mothers, then mothers become the emotional centers of the family. Fathers are isolated in families to the degree that they turn these tasks over to mothers. When the mother is in charge of these tasks, she is really in charge of the family. As we pointed out, none of these tasks require breast milk, and none actually rob men of their masculinity. But these tasks represent the fear of being "like mother" and the reaction of striving to be "not mother." This fear restrains men from the emotional closeness for which they married and raised children.

WHY FOCUS ATTENTION ON THESE DAY-TO-DAY FAMILY ACTIVITIES?

There are two reasons to stress the importance of these activities and the energy that it takes to follow through with them. The first reason directly affects fathers. In Chapter 2 we presented a structural view that illustrated a father's isolation in the traditional family. We emphasized the emotional isolation that fathers may experience. We reprint this illustration as Figure 8.1.

FIGURE 8.1. A Father's Isolation in a Family

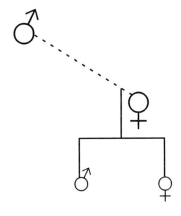

This emotional isolation is both created and maintained when all parenting tasks are assigned to mothers. In families, the day-to-day activities that we have described are antidotes to masculine depression. They require the opposites of dissociation, counterdependence, and self-focus—direct emotional experience, interdependence, and a focus on the emotional needs of others. Men who fully participate in these life-giving activities are able to develop interconnected and cooperative relationships, empathy, and an acceptance of feelings. In other words, they develop relational skills. Moreover, the man's acceptance of his children's and wife's feelings is intertwined with his reclaiming of his own emotional life. These two processes feed off each other.

In reality there is no reason why mothers are better equipped or should be the only ones to perform these activities, nurturing and maintaining family relationships by themselves. These activities require skills, and skills improve with time, practice, and commitment. To perform these family behaviors successfully, fathers need to develop the ability to be alert to the needs of others. They become invested in being part of something (as opposed to being all of something), understand a variety of emotional, social, and developmental needs of other people, and nurture the emerging needs of children. When fathers participate in these activities they cannot be isolated—emotionally, physically, or spiritually—from the family.

The second reason for emphasizing these everyday activities is the effect on families and cultures when fathers actively and naturally participate in child rearing. A son raised by a father who is as active a parent as his mother is not limited by traditional masculinity, as his identity is not based on antifemininity. He can achieve a comfortable masculinity because it is defined in positive terms, e.g., "I am like Dad." In cultures where fathers take equal responsibility for childrearing, there are fewer displays of aggression, violence, or other hypermasculine behaviors, and gender arrangements are more egalitarian. In terms of our model of masculinity, when fathers participate in childrearing, males do not need to dissociate from their feelings or act out in destructive and counterdependent ways. The energy that is currently expended maintaining the unnatural defense of traditional masculinity is naturally used in constructive ways in the multitude of tasks that are involved in raising healthy children.

WHAT DO TRADITIONAL MEN THINK
THAT CHILDREN NEED FROM THEM?

Fathers frequently rely on stereotyped gender role expectations to help fill in the gaps in their understanding of children. This tendency is especially evident in fathers' dealings with sons. The more that fathers have dissociated from their own feelings, the less they are able to have an empathic understanding of their children's needs. In place of empathy, fathers often rely on what they *think* children need. For some reason, fathers frequently think that children need to be tickled, tossed around, and teased.

Part of the "Dad Zone" is "play time." Fathers' interaction with children is frequently spent playing, and there is nothing wrong with this. If done appropriately, play with Father is fun, memorable, and nondestructive. However, if play time is the *only* time that fathers interact with children, other than in disciplinary interactions, then there is a continuation of the pattern of fathers failing to nurture and fully parent their children. Ultimately, this pattern maintains and can reproduce masculine depression.

Recent social trends have established the myth of "quality time"— the belief that parents do an adequate job if they interact intensively with children, even if they are frequently too busy to maintain much of a physical presence in their children's lives. However, the real problem is a lack of "quantity time." What children really need is for someone to be there for them and attend to their moment-to-moment physical and emotional needs—not every minute of the day, but often enough that they have a comfortable and ongoing relationship with the parent.

In a men's therapy group, a client described his father in the following way: "What I remember about my father is that, if I got up early enough, I could look out the window and see him driving off to work. If I stayed up late enough, I could still be awake when he came home. Sometimes he would play with me for fifteen minutes or so before bedtime." Clearly, those fifteen minutes were important to this man when he was a boy. This time is obviously better than nothing, but it does not substitute in any way for the frequent and regular contact that children crave.

A father's unmet needs for intimacy, coupled with his under-developed relational skills, may predispose him to subscribe to the myth of quality time, and to assume that quality time is the same as play time. Family activities require quantity time. Quality is reflected in the nature of the quantity time, i.e., the relational skills required in family activities. Quality time is inevitable, given quantity time and the commitment to learning about your child's emotional needs so that you can give them quality parenting. Conversely, quality time is impossible without quantity time. You can be entertaining with those whom you don't really know, but you can never form a real and intimate connection with them. The more that fathers are emotionally invested in families and attend to the tasks of family life, the more that they spend quality time with their families.

Relying on traditional masculinity and gender stereotypes as guides, fathers may think that what children need from them is help in "getting tough" and learning that "It's a tough world out there," and that the way to prepare for it is to attend less to feelings and more to competing. Fathers may fear that allowing for feelings and sensitivity will make children (especially boys) weak, fragile, and unable to cope with the rigors of living in a tough world.

CAN FATHERS NURTURE,
AND DOES NURTURING "SPOIL" CHILDREN?

The term "spoiling" refers to giving children too much of a good thing. Showering children with expensive gifts for no special reason or allowing them to be the center of attention at all times are behaviors that encourage children to be self-centered and discourage them from developing the emotional resources that they will need in order to be independent and interconnected with others. Nurturing involves attending to a child's emotional needs. It is very different from spoiling, which is a process by which someone gives a child something that is undeserved. All children deserve to be nurtured by virtue of the fact that they showed up on the planet. Children depend on their parents to make the world a safe place for them, to help them negotiate difficult developmental tasks, and to help them learn that they are valued and capable. Nurturing is vital to all of these processes.

There is a common misconception that nurturing and discipline are at opposite ends of a single continuum. People who subscribe to this misconception believe that one must withhold nurturing in order to apply discipline, and vice versa. Through the socialization and family processes we have described, men learn to value discipline to a much greater extent than they value nurturing. Feeling that they have to choose between the two, they frequently avoid nurturing and perhaps view it as dangerous (again, especially for sons). The view of nurturing and discipline as antithetical to each other severely limits men's parenting skills and facilitates the continuing patterns that result in masculine depression. Fathers tend to think that nurturing a child will leave him or her vulnerable to the harsh realities of the world, when in actuality, nurturing provides the child with the solid base of self-esteem necessary for coping in a difficult world.

In reality, nurturance and discipline are not an "either/or" decision. Parents can do more or less nurturing, and at the same time more or less disciplining, depending on the needs of the situation. Overreliance on one or the other has predictable outcomes. Consider the following diagram (see Figure 8.2).

We can see from this diagram that children need both nurturing and discipline. When parents consistently apply too little of either, children are affected in predictable and negative ways. A father's fear of femininity can severely limit his parenting skills by encouraging him to rely on discipline as his sole parenting tool. Children then experience their father as a stern taskmaster who, although he may care about them, does not ever show it. They feel fearful of his demands and deprived of his love. To the extent that sons identify with their fathers, they are at risk for continuing the behavior patterns that perpetuate masculine depression into the next generation.

WHAT DO CHILDREN
ACTUALLY NEED FROM FATHERS?

Children are constantly learning about themselves and the world. Unconsciously, they ask basic psychological questions: "Am I adequate and lovable?"; "Does making a mistake mean that I am bad or incompetent?"; "Should I feel ashamed of myself or can I feel comfortable with myself?"; "Can I trust my perceptions and abilities or is

FIGURE 8.2. Nurturance and Discipline in Parenting

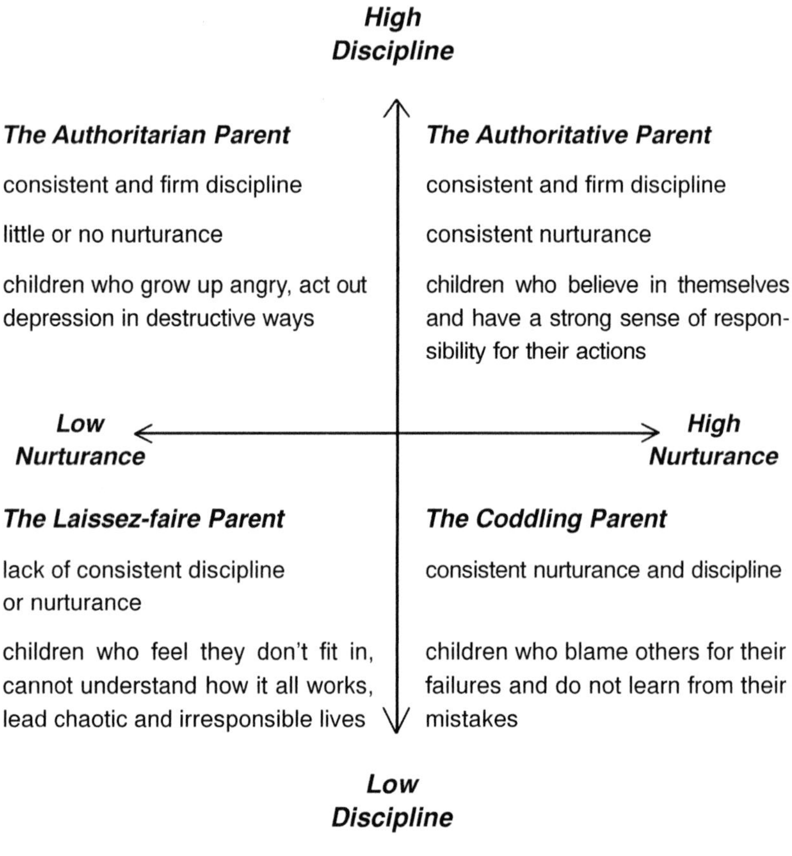

**High
Discipline**

The Authoritarian Parent

consistent and firm discipline

little or no nurturance

children who grow up angry, act out
depression in destructive ways

The Authoritative Parent

consistent and firm discipline

consistent nurturance

children who believe in themselves
and have a strong sense of responsibility for their actions

**Low
Nurturance** ←　　　　　→ **High
Nurturance**

The Laissez-faire Parent

lack of consistent discipline
or nurturance

children who feel they don't fit in,
cannot understand how it all works,
lead chaotic and irresponsible lives

The Coddling Parent

consistent nurturance and discipline

children who blame others for their
failures and do not learn from their
mistakes

**Low
Discipline**

there something wrong with me?"; or "Is the world a safe place or a
dangerous place?" Children cannot answer these and other basic questions for themselves. They do not even know that they are finding their
answers to these questions. Without empathy and understanding, fathers do not accurately comprehend the questions children ask, and
thus they cannot help children develop healthy answers. Children need
support, empathy, and understanding from an older, wiser adult. When
fathers exclusively give criticisms, corrections, or directions, children
may learn they are not adequate, and that they will need to depend on

others for help. Given the gendered ordering of the world, these inter-actions with their fathers often mean different things to a girl and a boy. The girl may grow up to search for a magic helper who will take over her life so that she does not have to deal directly with feelings of incompetence (she may be vulnerable to dominant and even violent partners). Given the cultural demands of masculinity, the boy is more likely to learn that he must never depend on anybody but himself, and thus he may learn to hide his fear of inadequacy by cultivating an appearance of autonomy and control, just like his dad. In either case, the child grows up ill-equipped to engage in a reciprocal and rich relationship, and thus he or she will have to settle for less, unless the sense of self that was lost in childhood can be reclaimed.

Children need the same empathic understanding and nurturance from fathers as they need, and obtain more often, from mothers. When children feel accepted and understood by someone as power-ful and competent as fathers appear to be, this experience can dra-matically boost children's self-esteem and trust in their adequacy and lovableness—"If both Dad and Mom love me and believe in me, then I must really be lovable and competent." When combined with nurturance, discipline is constructive and does not shame or humili-ate. Children grow both in self-esteem and a sense of responsibility for their behavior.

HOW CAN MEN STOP THE CYCLE
OF MASCULINE DEPRESSION?

Masculine depression results from the basic and faulty assumption that sensitivity and emotional expressiveness are the same as fragility and weakness. The irony is that the avoidance of emotional expres-siveness *creates* a covert weakness and fragility. When one has little emotional understanding or sophistication, strong feelings tend to be overwhelming. When men consistently avoid direct emotional expe-rience, feelings tend to come leaking out in the most distorted and inappropriate ways, resulting in damaged relationships and self-destructive behaviors. As we described in Chapter 4, the belief that feelings are a nuisance leaves men woefully unprepared to handle life situations where emotional issues are highlighted. Parenting fre-quently involves these kinds of situations.

Fathers can prevent masculine depression in their sons by overcoming their own fear of feeling and emotional expressiveness, by accepting their sons' sensitivity and feelings, and by believing that feelings strengthen people and relationships. Fathers can do these things by fully participating in child rearing, overcoming their own need to hide feelings, and allowing their sensitivity to develop into the empathy that allows their sons and daughters to feel loved, encouraged, and accepted. This seems like a tall order, but again, it involves learning a set of skills that improve with practice. Men understand the metaphor that if you do not show up for the game, or if you stay on the sidelines, you will never get to play in the game. Masculine depression keeps fathers on the sidelines, in the other room, or in the "Dad Zone." Families function best when everyone is playing on the same team.

Fathers can parent sons to prevent masculine depression through three basic processes: nurturing, modeling, and teaching. We have already described the value of nurturing, which communicates to a child that his or her emotional experiences are important and valuable. The other two processes of modeling and teaching also impress on sons the strength, value, and honesty of full emotional expression.

Modeling involves teaching by example. The more that fathers participate in the complex and ever-evolving activities that define family life, the more that fathers teach sons to be fully human. As fathers live a life without dissociating from their feelings or losing their awareness of the needs of others, they help their sons to resist the cultural pressures to be like everyone else and adopt destructive masculinity in order to provide an artificial sense of safety in an ambiguous world.

When a child becomes old enough to understand more complex concepts, fathers can augment this modeling by talking to their sons about the negative side of traditional masculinity, the choices that men have about accepting or rejecting it, and the consequences of these choices. When children become aware of gender pressure, they gain an important tool for resisting it.

HOW DO ISOLATED FATHERS
AFFECT DAUGHTERS?

(Note: This book is not intended to fully explore or do justice to the complexities of women's issues. We mention girls' development only in this limited perspective to emphasize the importance of fathers' participation in child rearing, to briefly highlight the limiting effects of traditional masculinity on female development, and to point out that traditional masculinity starts and is maintained in family relationships.)

Daughters have internalized images of both parents. In the problematic family, these images are of an overfunctioning mother and an isolated, disconnected father. Fathers present the same appearance to daughters as they do to sons. The only real difference is that fathers are the adult representation of the other sex. Daughters are potentially affected in two ways. First, they see and internalize an image of an emotionally connected and overfunctioning mother. Consciously and unconsciously, daughters learn about being a woman. Due to mother's emotional accessibility daughters may learn more about what being female *is*, (as opposed to boys learning about what masculinity *is not*). Girls may develop more clear models of mother's overfunctioning in family activities and mother's participation in behaviors that subtly support male domestic limitations.

As girls learn about femininity from their mothers, they learn about masculinity from their fathers. Daughters may come to expect males to be emotionally inaccessible and domestically limited. They may not fully realize that they have the right to expect emotional access and full domestic partnership from a male. As daughters grow to become women and, often, wives, these expectations become powerful influences in subtle and unconscious life choices.

WHAT IS THE MOST DESTRUCTIVE EXPERIENCE THAT FATHERS CAN HELP SONS AVOID?

There are many ways in which a father becomes an absent parent and displays the unrealistic image that leads a son to think of masculinity only in its extreme forms. Most of this parenting is passive. Father is not usually going out of his way to demonstrate masculinity to his son. He is simply "doing" masculinity, and his son is watching.

When fathers are limited by traditional masculinity, and when they are passive in parenting their sons, they rely on the same destructive behaviors that they learned during the course of their own development. Traditional masculinity does not emphasize empathy or nurturing, but healthy parenting requires these qualities. When fathers have not healed the hurtful experiences of their own development, they tend to pass similar experiences on to their sons.

The main mechanism for actively transmitting masculine depression from fathers to sons is shame. A father shames his son when he actively lets the son know that his father is not proud of him because the son is not behaving in masculine (valued) ways.

Eight-year-old Jackie was learning how to hit a baseball in little league, but he was having difficulty because he was afraid that the ball would hit him. So he backed away as soon as the ball was pitched. His father, the coach, said to him, "Come on, you sissy, stand in there and hit it!" Jackie felt ashamed and inadequate. His father had let him know, in no uncertain terms, that he was disappointed in Jackie's lack of masculinity.

Passive fathering is harmful in that an absent father begins a boy's futile search for masculinity. Destructively active fathering sends powerful shaming messages to boys about their inadequacy. Once fears of inadequacy begin, they tend to remain hidden, as traditional masculinity prevents boys from revealing their fears or weaknesses. The effects of shameful experiences with fathers are manifested in masculine depression in sons.

Thus, fathers should avoid creating the experience of worthlessness in children. As this feeling can be produced by either psychological absence or by shaming, fathers can avoid this most destructive experience by being present both physically and psychologically, and by never using humiliation as a motivator. In the case of sons, shame can create a humiliation that is tied to his masculinity. The feeling of masculine inadequacy has been tied to aggressive and self-destructive behaviors. In fact, it is a predictor of sexual assault perpetration. Boys who grow up feeling unvalued by their fathers are at risk for lashing out at women in order to defend against their own feelings of inadequacy. (Please note that these feelings are a risk factor, not an inevitable path to sexual aggression.)

Many fathers feel as if they should parent their children like stereotypical football coaches—harsh, uncaring, challenging, and humiliating. They fear that their sons will not achieve their full potential if they do not provide all of these. In reality, challenge is the only positive one of these four behaviors. Parents (and football coaches, for that matter) use humiliation when they do not know how to provide challenge in a positive manner. Children can be high achievers when they are challenged, encouraged, and nurtured. Effective parents do this with their children (just as *good* coaches do this with their players).

ARE MOTHERS AND FATHERS THE SAME OR DIFFERENT?

By now you may have predicted our response. In healthy families, both parents are capable of performing all of the parenting duties: nurturing, discipline, physical care, maintenance tasks, and all of the behaviors that allow a family to function on a daily basis. Splitting the parenting tasks along stereotypical gender lines has the effect of limiting the child's conception of the possibilities of male and female. Traditional masculinity takes men far from relationship and nurturing skills, and it forces women to compensate for limited masculine domestic abilities. The more that children come to rely solely on mothers, the more that fathers are isolated and underdeveloped. Fathers need to feel *more special* in the lives of their families, but they can only do so by being *less different* from mothers.

WHAT ARE THE ABCs OF CHANGE?

Affect
>—have empathy, experience your own feelings, be patient with yourself.

Behavior
>—leave the "Dad Zone" and fully participate in nurturant child rearing.

Cognition
>—understand that sensitivity is strength and connection, not weakness.

Remember that emotional skills improve with practice.

Chapter 9

Fear and Rage
in the Lives of Men

In the summer of 1993, worldwide news media covered a sensational story of a Virginia couple, John and Lorena Bobbitt. Theirs was a marriage fraught with frequent and violent conflict. Late on a June night, after a particularly intense confrontation, Lorena cut off John's penis with a kitchen knife while he was sleeping.

In the aftermath of this tragedy, Lorena Bobbitt claimed that she was the victim of years of severe emotional, physical, and sexual abuse by her husband. On the night she severed his penis, she said that John had raped her, and that he did so often.

There was little question that John had been violent toward Lorena. Police records described several previous incidents. A few months following the couple's divorce, John was again arrested in a domestic violence incident, this time involving his new girlfriend. While John has not been convicted of any crime (and, in fact, he was found not guilty of marital rape following the original incident), there is ample evidence to suggest that this is a man who habitually behaves violently toward his partner.

A year later, in June 1994, the world was again stunned when former football great O. J. Simpson was charged in the double murder of his ex-wife, Nicole, and her friend, Ronald Goldman. Again, police records indicated a history of violence in the home. Some years before, O. J. had pleaded no contest to a charge of assaulting Nicole. He was directed to attend counseling sessions, pay a small fine, and perform some community service. After he was charged with murder, news media obtained the release of audiotapes of emergency telephone calls from Nicole to the police during earlier incidents. On these tapes, she is clearly in fear of being hurt by this man, who can be heard ranting in the background. Whether or not O. J. Simpson committed these murders, it was clear that this is a violent man, and that the target of his rage was his ex-wife.

These two incidents sensitized the public to the serious problem of men's violence against their wives. Former Surgeon General C. Everett Koop called domestic violence the most serious health problem for U.S. women, as it kills or injures more women than breast cancer and accidents combined.[1] This estimation of the problem is shared by Robert McAfee, president of the American Medical Association.[2] About one-quarter of women's emergency hospital visits, suicides, and requests for emergency psychiatric services are tied to domestic violence.[3] A particularly chilling fact is that 30 percent of female homicide victims are murdered by their partners or ex-partners.[4] Women are more likely to be raped on a date or by their husbands than they are if they are walking down a dark alley late at night.[5] An American woman is abused by her partner on the average of once every fifteen seconds,[6] and domestic violence costs billions of dollars annually in law enforcement costs, health care expenses, and lost work time.[7]

In this chapter, we focus on the problem of violence in intimate relationships. Men's abuse of their wives is related to many of the themes we have presented: depression, narcissism, traditional masculinity, and anger. We begin with an exploration of the latter, as anger often (but not always) precedes wife beating. We will then turn to a description of the psychological world of the batterer and to strategies for men to use in avoiding physical violence.

We will develop two major themes in our discussion of anger:

- anger provides information, and
- anger usually reflects other feelings.

WHAT ANGER IS

Anger is a feeling that, like all feelings, provides information. Anger tells us that we need to *protect ourselves* from some sort of danger—physical or psychological, real or imagined. For example, we may sense a threat to our physical safety, self-esteem, financial resources, moral standards, or other important aspects of our lives. When we feel angry, we are alerted to the presence of something we need to remove or change in order to re-establish our safety.

WHAT ANGER IS NOT

Many people confuse anger with violence. While these two things often occur together, they do not have a direct connection. Anger is a *feeling*. Violence is a *behavior*. While anger may be a reaction, violence is a *decision*. Anger serves the function of alerting us to threat; violence is one way of dealing with that threat—by harming or destroying it. There may be instances where violence is an appropriate response to anger, such as when someone is physically assaulting us or someone we care about. Except in this circumstance, it is difficult to imagine instances in the home where violent behavior is appropriate. Yet, many men beat their wives and children when the reasoned expression of anger escalates into its frenzied, panic-driven form—rage. In addition, some men who are not physically violent engage in a kind of psychological violence—bullying, neglect, and other forms of emotional abuse.

HOW DOES THE EXPRESSION OF ANGER BECOME SO DISTORTED?

Anger can be protective and constructive, as we described in Chapter 7. For example, one can say to one's partner, "I care and trust you enough to let you know what is really bothering me. If you can understand why I am angry and help me to deal with it, we can be much closer." Relationships improve when partners pay attention to their anger and share it with each other in constructive ways.

Anger is rarely present by itself. As we mentioned in Chapter 5, fear and hurt often accompany it. But traditional masculinity does not allow the full expression of these vulnerable feelings, therefore, fear and hurt are often dissociated from awareness, leaving only the conscious experience of anger. Anger becomes rage because of the perceived level of danger presented by the threat and the limited expression of hurt or fear. Many men are not able to say, "I am afraid that she will leave me, and I know that if she does, I will be devastated. My masculine sense of self will be shattered, so I will beat her to stop her from leaving and make her feel that it is all her fault." However, these are exactly the hurts and fears behind domestic violence. When men cannot express these feelings in conscious and constructive ways, they express them in dissociated and destructive ways.

As an example, a relationship breakup involves a powerful experience of emotional loss, and one must assimilate that loss into one's sense of self in order to recover healthy functioning. This course of recovery from loss is known as *grieving*. It is a process by which one expresses, works through, eventually accepts the feelings that have accompanied the loss, and comes to a point of resolution that allows one to move on with one's life.

Grieving has a life of its own. It is quite natural to feel and behave in certain ways—such as crying, reminiscing, and expressing a wish that one had treated the person better—in response to loss. Every culture has funeral rituals that help people to initiate the grief process following the ultimate loss, death. The grieving process takes time; one cannot spend an hour grieving and be done with it once and for all. Depending on the loss, it can take months or even years. The man who has lost his partner is aware that something is wrong, but many men avoid grieving because it involves the expression of vulnerable feelings, and also involves acknowledging that he feels connected to her. These two behaviors are culturally defined as unmasculine, and so he tends to make efforts to distract himself so that he does not have to deal with his pain. He pays a price for doing so, as he is likely to develop symptoms, which are his body's and his mind's way of telling him that something is wrong. If he does not heed these signals, he will continue to have these symptoms. When there comes a time for him to again become involved in a relationship, he will be predisposed to acting out the psychological issues that arise from an incomplete grieving process.

HOW IS LACK OF EMPATHY FOR THE SELF RELATED TO DOMESTIC VIOLENCE?

Psychologist David Lisak coined the term *empathy for the self* in his work with male victims of childhood abuse. As we mentioned earlier, some of these men become perpetrators of violence as adults. Lisak's research indicated that those men who were able to acknowledge the emotional and physical pain of their experience as victims showed a strong tendency to not become violent as adults. In contrast, those who dissociated and denied their pain tended to later act it out in a violent way.[8] Being able to understand one's own vulnerable feelings—having empathy for the self—allowed one to have empathy for other people, and thus not harm them.

While the man who batters may appear to be the epitome of traditional masculinity, his inner life is completely the opposite. He feels that he can never be a "real man"—that he will never be accepted and revered as truly masculine. Because he has fully accepted the traditional masculine value system, this felt sense contributes powerfully to a deep-seated but usually unconscious sense of worthlessness. Like the schoolyard bully, the only way he can feel worthwhile, even for a short time, is to raise himself by lowering others. Like most destructive masculine behavior, domestic violence is counterphobic and compensatory. Men do not commit violence so much because they want to be powerful as because they feel *powerless* and need to counteract this very uncomfortable emotional experience.

Our position is that virtually all men have experienced at least mild forms of abuse as children—harsh, masculine demands to not feel, acknowledge pain, or be connected to others. The same processes that Lisak saw so dramatically with victims of extreme abuse can be seen to a lesser extent with anybody—people who acknowledge their own vulnerability are respectful and supportive when others are vulnerable.

Many men are physically or psychologically violent in relationships because they lack empathy for themselves, and as a result, they lack empathy for others. They cannot recognize their own hurt and fear and are driven to protect themselves from feelings of powerlessness by being violent. Their frenzied and destructive behavior obliterates any awareness of the terror and fear that they inflict on their victims. When negative emotional experience is coupled with the masculine demand to deny all feeling, the combination is a volatile one. In order to have successful intimate relationships that are free of emotional and psychological violence, men must learn to recognize and understand their own feelings so that they can become capable of doing the same with the feelings of their partners.

Appropriate empathy for self allows for healthy grieving, which is an expression of feelings. Avoiding or denying grieving, which involves dissociating from feelings, can lead to such destructive behaviors as violence.

Lisak also did extensive interviews with men who admitted to committing another closely associated violent crime, acquaintance rape. In contrast to control subjects, these men had strikingly negative feelings about their fathers. They tended to see their fathers as demanding and uncaring. The sons exhibited a chronic sense of not being able to measure up as a man. They were victims of emotional (and sometimes physical) abuse, who, as adults, attempted to prove their virility and act out their rage by committing acts of violence against women.[9]

Other research by Lisak has revealed that men who have been abused in some way as children *and* have accepted masculinity's traditional values are more likely to become violent adults, in comparison to other men who have been abused as children. His contention is that, as children, these men have experienced powerful and painful emotional events. At the same time, they have absorbed the social message that expressing vulnerable feelings is taboo for males—the classic "big boys don't cry" dictum. These boys find that they can follow one of two paths: they can reject traditional masculinity and deal with the tragedy of their victimization, or they can accept it and act out their intense rage by becoming abusive themselves. Violence appears to lie at the confluence of victimization and the demands of traditional masculinity.[10]

The man who is violent in the home feels unloved and worthless, but he cannot tolerate or express these feelings. He deals with them by projecting them outside of himself, on to some safe object, and then controlling the hated part of the self by crushing his victim. Objects are safe when they are smaller and weaker. He cannot feel empathy for his victims because he is so unaware of his own feelings of shame and vulnerability. In other words, it is impossible for a person to feel for others when his own emotional life is impoverished. He has no frame of reference for emotional pain because his defenses against his own pain are so rigid.

Masculine development emphasizes action, not emotion. When a man feels sad, hurt, or worried, traditional masculinity encourages him to convert his feelings into the culturally acceptable masculine reaction, anger, and to *do* something about the problem in order to change the way he feels. For many men, feelings become a problem to get rid of instead of a source of valuable information about their deeper needs. Masculine narcissism can result in punishing other people for "causing" these feelings.

HOW IS DOMESTIC VIOLENCE RELATED TO MEN'S ASSUMPTIONS ABOUT GENDER?

It is clear from crime reports that domestic violence has a great deal to do with being male.[11] It is also clear from research studies that domestic violence has a great deal to do with being traditionally masculine. Compared with nonviolent men, batterers tend to be overconforming to the traditional masculine gender role. Thus they hold ideologies about relationships and have feelings about themselves that encourage violence.[12]

One traditional gender ideology is that women are the property of men and therefore should be under men's control. Rather than seeing his wife as a partner, the batterer tends to see her as an underling (a narcissistic extension) whom he supports in exchange for domestic, sexual, and other services. When she fails to conform to his wishes, he feels the need to assert control. Violence, threats, and intimidation seem to be excellent means of doing so, especially for the man who lacks social and relationship skills. He overconforms to traditionally masculine values that sanction or even glorify such behavior. Her failure to conform to his demands is inevitable—she wants to have her own power and may react negatively to her his frequent subordination of her.

Traditional men are expected to be powerful and in control of their situations, and it is no surprise that the research indicates that batterers exhibit a higher need for power and control than their nonviolent counterparts. Violence against the partner seems to be not so much in the service of increasing power, but more in reaction to the perceived threat of *loss* of power. As the partner asserts herself, he feels less in control and feels the need to assert himself in the only way he knows. Domestic violence seems to be a kind of "preemptive strike" against feelings of powerlessness.

Repeated violence against his partner often allows a man to gain control over her behavior and her life. She becomes fearful of expressing her opinions or doing anything without his permission, and he may also control her economically. Some research indicates that victims actually begin to perceive themselves as having fewer options than they really have.[13] As a result, their behavior, already restricted by their partners, becomes further narrowed by this distorted perception. Some of her perceptions, however, may be quite realistic. Evidence suggests that women who move out of abusive situations increase the likelihood that they will be injured seriously or murdered by their ex-partners.[14]

WHAT ARE THE STAGES
OF DOMESTIC VIOLENCE?

We will review two processes related to the stages of domestic violence—one involving the violent man's behavior; the other involving his conflicted feelings about his relationship with his partner. These reactions cycle through patterns of change in relation to each other. Both are related to the other psychological conflicts that we discussed previously, especially the masculine dilemma, "not too close, not too far away." The man's behavioral changes within the relationship reflect fluctuations in his emotional world.

Research indicates that batterers fall into two basic categories: generally violent men and "jealous husband" types.[15] The former group is made up of men who have strong sociopathic tendencies. Their violence against their partners is a part of a general pattern of violence in many aspects of their lives. These men are more severely disturbed than the other type and frequently end up with long prison sentences. For our purposes, we will discuss the more common type of batterer, the jealous husband type, whose violence is more directly related to many of the themes that we have developed: masculine depression, masculine narcissism, and the masculine dilemma in relationships.

For these men, the relational behaviors of domestic violence generally follow a cycle. Although there are variations in how long or intense any part of the cycle may be, the overall pattern is fairly consistent. Most abusive relationships do not start out violently; both partners are intent on making a good impression, creating an emotional bond, and attending to the other person. This is the *honeymoon* phase of the relationship. Conflicts are downplayed, and the joys of new love dominate interactions.

This peaceful, even loving and committed period gives way to a gradual increase in tension and conflict. Anxiety and a buildup of anger replace love and affection. Every problem seems to develop into a crisis.

When tension and anxiety reach a peak, a crisis phase ensues, and the man becomes violent. The batterer's behavior is explosive and unpredictable, and he tends to blame the victim for the problem. She may accommodate her behavior to his wishes in order to survive and/or she may submit to his abuse because she sees no other option.

When the crisis has passed, the couple reenters a calm phase. Both are relieved that the violence and rage are over. The abuser may become extremely remorseful and loving, begging for his partner's forgiveness, promising to never be violent again, being very considerate, expressing his caring for her, and even showering her with gifts. She is so worn down by the crisis and relieved at its passing, that she may accept his promises and presents. She may feel wonderful to be needed so desperately. Unfortunately, this is usually only a way station in the cycle of abuse. The tension and crisis phases are almost sure to follow again, unless there is intervention.

This repetitive pattern of behavior reflects a repetitive pattern of conflict within the man, specifically the man's attachment-separation problems reflected in the masculine dilemma of "not too close, not too far away." During the honeymoon phase, attachment needs predominate. If this is a new relationship, he may be coming out of a lengthy time in which he felt unloved and empty. Being cared for feels very relieving and fulfilling as his previously unmet dependency needs are temporarily satisfied. If this is a calm phase following an abusive crisis, he feels close to his partner again after a period of emotional alienation. Again, the relief of filling his primitive attachment needs allows him to downplay his ambivalence toward the woman. In either case, he feels close to her, but not too close.

But these dependency needs become problematic during the tension phase. Now his attachment to her feels like a threat to his masculine self. He begins to feel that she is a burden, or that she really does not love him. Increasingly, she seems to make him angry, and he has little patience for her. Now he is feeling too close, and he adopts several strategies to put some interpersonal distance between them. Among these distancing strategies are denial of his own vulnerability, exaggeration of his dependence, passive-aggressive behaviors such as chronic lateness and irresponsibility, and emotional maltreatment of his partner.

These strategies do not work, however, and he becomes increasingly more uncomfortable. Meanwhile, his distancing attempts are causing his partner discomfort, thus bringing more stress into the relationship. At some point, his rage at his own dependence becomes unbearable, and he lashes out violently at her. This outburst allows him to purge his negative feelings and act out the negative side of his ambivalence toward her, but this emotional release obviously comes at a price. His wife is now afraid, angry, and alienated from him. She may leave him or threaten to leave him, and he comes to a realization of how much he needs her. Now he feels too far away and, confronted with his own dependency, he takes desperate steps to keep her—apologizing, gift giving, etc. If he is "successful," she stays and they re-enter the honeymoon phase. If she leaves him, he may become conventionally depressed (as we saw with Bobby in Chapter 8), or he may stalk her, as he is confronted not only with his dependence, but with his lack of control over someone whom he believes should be under his control.

Not surprisingly, perpetrators of domestic violence tend to come from homes in which they witnessed and/or were the victims of the same kind of behavior. Because their fathers and stepfathers often beat their mothers, their early experience was that this kind of behavior was a normal way of handling conflict and solving problems within the family. Importantly, they also may have observed their fathers being rewarded for violence—by compliance and reestablished control.

ARE POWER STRUGGLES RELATED TO DOMESTIC VIOLENCE?

Yes. Changes in the power dynamics of a relationship precipitate many instances of domestic violence. Her exercise of power or autonomy threatens his sense of masculine adequacy, as his experience of being a powerful man depends entirely on her being a subservient woman. When his power is threatened by her assertiveness and his emotional expression is limited by traditional masculinity, he frequently resorts to some form of violence in order to resolve the power struggle. Men need to recognize these struggles and develop healthy responses to them, as we discussed in Chapter 7.

WHAT KINDS OF SOCIAL CHANGES
WOULD DECREASE DOMESTIC VIOLENCE?

The lengthy tradition of tolerating the male abuse of their wives and children has resulted in a lack of accountability for individual men. One critical part of the puzzle is to repair the systems that hold these men responsible for their own behavior. Obviously, the criminal justice system is a major one. Incarceration is necessary for the repeat or severe offender in order to keep him from doing further damage. We need more research into and development of effective treatment programs. There is no contradiction between understanding the roots of domestic violence and holding men responsible for their behavior.

The very fabric of masculinity is interwoven with demands for aggression and the denial of one's emotional life. Take a careful look at violent masculinity in the culture—football, boxing, action-adventure movies, "cop shows," war mongering. All of these both reflect and sustain men's violence.

The mitigation of the problem is an arduous process, but several strategies are available. First, education needs to give a clear message to men and boys that domestic violence is not normal, natural, or tolerable. Schools need to teach this with attention paid to the gender-based encouragement of violence. Colleges need to support men's studies so that men can understand themselves not merely as generic human beings, but as people who have feelings and reactions to their masculinity.

Men must take more responsibility for the gender education of males. Domestic violence is too often described as a "women's issue." There is a social assumption that male aggression is inevitable, and that therefore we should only concentrate on victims. If men speak out against male violence, we can start to change the destructive culture of masculinity. We present some strategies for social change in Chapter 10.

Domestic violence is a complex problem that has its roots in social inequality, masculine psychology, dysfunctional family dynamics, faulty gender ideologies, masculine depression, and the childhood victimization of males. We return to the title of Chapter 3: "Inhumane Treatment Leads to Inhuman Behavior." Violence is the worst kind of inhuman behavior, and it will stop when men recover their full humanity and help other men to do the same. One of the most troubling aspects of the O. J. Simpson case is that no prominent sports figures spoke out publicly about Simpson's domestic violence, and there is no evidence that any of his close male friends spoke privately to him about it. Nobody violated the "fraternity rules." As we said in Chapter 6, it is crucial that men stand up and say, "This is wrong. Stop it!"

Violent men have a responsibility to their families and themselves to deal with their feelings in more constructive ways. Nonviolent men have a responsibility to other men and society to use their considerable influence with one another to make the kinds of positive changes that will result in a better quality of life for everyone.

WHAT ARE THE ABCs OF CHANGE?

Affect
   —recover the experience of the vulnerable feelings that accompany anger.

Behavior
   —express your vulnerable feelings appropriately.
   —express disapproval for men's violence.

Cognition
   —"I feel angry; what vulnerability is underneath?"
   —"I can control my anger."

Chapter 10

The Big Picture

We hope that we have helped you to think about men's behavior in a new way, based on a gendered view of depression. Unfortunately, masculine depression is not only destructive in the context of emotional relationships. It also damages men's physical health and lowers the quality of both men's and women's lives. In this chapter, we will speak both descriptively and prescriptively about men's physical health issues. Then, we will step into the widest possible definition of health, that of prevention and social change, and describe ways in which men can contribute to changing destructive gender patterns in the world.

Health is obviously very important to everyone's quality of life. We will focus on the physiological aspects of health, which are intertwined with emotional aspects. Our emotional lives influence our physical well-being and vice versa. Modern medicine and health psychology are exploring the cutting edge of this connection, and we will review some of the literature in these areas.

We have explored ways in which men can improve the quality of their lives as well as the lives of those around them, but we cannot neglect the fact that physical problems can make the emotional tasks that we have described more difficult. It would seem to go without saying, but it is impossible for a man to address masculine depression, the vitality of his primary relationship, or the developmental needs of his children, if he is dead.

We apologize for having stated it so bluntly, but this alarming fact is worth repeating: men die an average of seven years earlier than women. Many of these premature deaths are tied to behaviors associated with destructive masculinity, such as unnecessary risk taking or bottling up angry feelings.[1] These deaths are therefore preventable. Men need to actively take care of their physical and emotional health to fulfill their commitments to themselves, their wives, and their children. Powerful cultural and psychological forces sometimes restrain them from doing so.

In this chapter, we review the literature on the male-female longevity difference, describe the factors contributing to this difference, discuss the connections between masculine depression and an array of men's health problems, and make recommendations for men who are interested in improving their health practices. Then, we expand the frame of healing in masculine depression to include ways that men can contribute to the social change that will decrease destructive masculinity and the resulting masculine depression in the culture at large.

WHAT IS THE DIFFERENCE IN LONGEVITY BETWEEN MALES AND FEMALES?

In the United States, the average gender difference in longevity hovers around seven years, although we see some minor variations in U.S. Bureau of the Census data from year to year. Compared with females, males are at stronger risk for premature and preventable death, and ethnic minority males are especially vulnerable. [2]

Despite the social belief that men are stronger, healthier, and hardier than women, males die at higher rates than females at every stage of life, beginning at conception. Twice as many women as men survive beyond age eighty, and eleven out of twelve U.S. wives outlive their husbands.[3]

Male lung cancer deaths exceed women's by a ratio of six to one, cirrhosis of the liver by two to one.[4] Although roughly equal numbers of men and women die of heart disease, men tend to die at much younger ages.[5] Men are three times more likely to die in motor vehicle accidents.[6] They commit suicide four times more often[7] and are victims of homicide in much greater numbers than women.[8] In fact, men have higher death rates for all fifteen leading causes of death.[9]

WHAT ARE THE CAUSES OF MEN'S HEALTH PROBLEMS?

It is difficult to separate biological and psychological causes of health problems because biology affects behavior and vice versa. For example, certain hereditary factors may predispose a man toward heart disease, but he can also negatively affect his heart by being chronically angry, eating the wrong foods, and failing to exercise. A complete discussion of all of the research on men's health problems is beyond the scope of this book. We will describe the major findings in the areas of the physical and the psychological.

One obvious place to look for the causes of sex differences in longevity is in the differences in male and female biology—genes and hormones. For instance, hemophilia is a life-threatening disorder that is linked to a recessive X chromosome gene for which there is no corresponding gene on the shorter Y chromosome. Females, who have two X chromosomes, are much less likely to contract this disease. However, most genetic sex-linked health problems are not life threatening. Baldness, color blindness, and (some researchers speculate) dyslexia are examples.[10] Hormonal differences probably serve to shorten men's lives, as testosterone appears to have a negative effect (and estrogen a positive effect) on cholesterol,[11] a major factor in heart disease, which is the number one cause of death throughout the world.[12]

Although there is little doubt that men are biologically more vulnerable than women, a great number of health problems can be attributed to the social pressure to be masculine—to ignore safety concerns, avoid opportunities for social support, restrict one's emotions, engage in dangerous sports, etc. Consider the following lengthy list. Men are more likely than women to:

- eat foods with poor nutritional value
- use tobacco products
- play dangerous sports such as football and boxing
- do "weekend warrior" kinds of exercise that are highly strenuous (this style of exercising actually increases one's risk of heart attack)
- refuse to use sunscreen
- drink and drive
- abuse alcohol and other drugs
- commit suicide
- avoid or delay seeing a physician for health problems or regular checkups
- engage in unsafe sexual practices
- work in hazardous environments

- refuse to take time off from work when sick
- fail to learn about health behaviors (such as recognizing the signs of prostate cancer or doing testicular self-examination)
- be physically violent
- neglect to use seat belts[13]

All of these health risks involve behaviors (or nonbehaviors), thus they are changeable in ways that genes and hormones are not.

HOW ARE HEALTH
AND TRADITIONAL MASCULINITY RELATED?

Men who endorse traditional and stereotypical attitudes about masculinity are significantly more likely to take health risks and die earlier than those with less stereotypical gender beliefs. Traditional masculinity and the resulting masculine depression has quite literally killed millions of men. There are at least four ways in which psychological processes related to masculinity can contribute to health problems:

- direct self-destructive behaviors,
- neglect of health needs,
- taking physical risks, and
- hurting oneself indirectly through destructive emotional processes.

WHAT KINDS OF DIRECT SELF-DESTRUCTIVE
BEHAVIORS DO MEN FREQUENTLY ENGAGE IN?

Direct self-destruction involves behaviors that cause damage to the body in a straightforward way. The two major direct self-destructive causes of death are substance abuse—including tobacco, alcohol, and other drugs—and suicide.

One of the largest factors in the seven-year male-female longevity difference is the sex difference in the use of tobacco products, the only legally available commodities in the United States that, when used as intended, will likely result in the death of the user if given enough time. Health problems associated with tobacco use (including cigar smoking and "smokeless" tobacco) are well-documented: emphysema, asthma, bronchitis, and various forms of cancer.[14] The average age at which males begin chewing tobacco or using snuff is age nine![15] There is a long tradition in advertising of associating tobacco use with masculinity. The Marlboro Man is probably the best example—a rugged cowboy who enjoys smoking cigarettes in the wide open spaces. (Ironically, one of the first models who played the Marlboro Man died of lung cancer and made public statements prior to his death begging people to stop smoking.)

Excessive drug use (including alcohol, the most abused drug in the world), is another example of direct self-damaging behavior. Sex differences in substance abuse and dependence vary according to age and ethnic group, but in every case, men have higher rates than women, ranging from a ratio of two to one to seven to one.[16] It is estimated that alcohol abuse and addiction are associated with up to 15 percent of *all* health care costs, lowered work productivity, suicide risk, automobile accidents, domestic violence, and divorce. Depression is a strong risk factor for substance abuse problems.[17]

Suicide is the ultimate self-destructive act. Although females *attempt* suicide more often, males *complete* suicides four times more often than females in the United States. This ratio is even more lopsided at adolescence and old age.[18] An understanding of the pressures of masculinity sheds light on these statistics.

Teenage girls make 75 percent of all suicide attempts within this age range, but boys make 80 percent of all completed suicides.[19] If we look at the interaction of adolescence and gender demands for males, we can speculate about one of the causes of teenage male suicide. Gender demands are especially highlighted in adolescence. It is the time of the football captain, the homecoming queen, the senior prom, and the overemphasis of gender stereotypes in dating and sex. Living up to masculine demands is extremely important to most teenage boys, yet they are socially proscribed from talking with each other about this pressure. You will never hear adolescent boys saying, "I'm not so sure of myself as a man, are you? Maybe we should ask your dad." Instead, they tend to posture with each other in an attempt to present an image of self-confidence and masculine adequacy. Those boys who feel like failures in living up to gender demands may be at risk for suicide.

Two particular groups of adolescent boys are especially at risk.[20] Boys who have experienced childhood physical, emotional, and sexual abuse have had powerful, negative, vulnerable emotional experiences. They may find it quite difficult to feel self-confident, in control, or independent. The second group is gay males, who, because of our homophobic society, witness denigration and outright attack on an important part of their identities on a daily basis.

Both groups of boys become aware, at some level, that they will never live up to the social demands of masculinity, because they have socially defined "feminine" experience. For the abused boy, it is the experience of the strong vulnerable emotion and the out-of-control experience of being victimized physically, emotionally, and/or sexually. He knows that he was unable to be masculine and defend himself. He has two wounds—the original abuse and the failure to defend himself as males are supposed to do. For the gay boy, what could be more "feminine" than loving a male? Gay male teenagers seek love and acceptance from other boys of their age group, who often shame and abuse gays and lesbians. The social demands may be so powerful that these perceived masculine "failures" can be an important factor in suicidal behavior.

Suicide among elderly men is reaching epidemic proportions.[21] Even the man who has been successful in the masculine world may find it difficult to continue to do so when he reaches old age. At this time of life, he is becoming physically weaker. He may need to ask for help more often. He finds himself more frequently in the socially defined women's sphere of influence, the home. He may retire, thus losing the all-important masculine work role, or experience a downturn in his productivity at work. In short, all of the traditional masculine trappings tend to fall away in old age. Old men who attempt to maintain the "macho" image are emotionally unprepared for the challenges that aging brings. They may assume that their usefulness as a male, i.e., solving problems and providing income, is over. Rather than face the prospect of redefining the self in a more relational (feminine) way, a significant group of men choose suicide as a masculine solution to their emotional pain. They would rather die than be considered unmasculine.

WHAT KINDS OF POSITIVE HEALTH BEHAVIORS DO MEN FREQUENTLY AVOID?

One can passively damage one's health by neglecting to perform certain behaviors, such as seeing a physician when ill or for regular checkups, taking necessary medication, paying attention to nutritional and exercise needs, using seat belts, and heeding symptoms of cancer or other serious problems. Between 30 percent and 50 percent of hypertension (high blood pressure) patients stop taking their medication, causing an increased risk of heart attack.[22] Most of these patients are men. Enlarged prostate affects half of all males over the age of fifty, yet many men delay treatment for this very uncomfortable condition for years and years.[23] A large number of men also undermine potential lifesaving treatment for prostate or colorectal cancer by ignoring symptoms or delaying treatment.[24] When they seek treatment, they tend to underreport their symptoms.[25] Male physicians ask male patients fewer questions than they ask females. Male physicians are especially reluctant to talk with male patients about problems related to bowel, bladder, and sexual functioning.[26]

WHAT KINDS OF RISKY HEALTH BEHAVIORS ARE COMMON IN MEN?

A third way to compromise one's health is to engage in behaviors that put one in potentially dangerous situations. The most obvious risky behaviors include: drunk driving, playing dangerous sports, being physically aggressive, provoking fights, or engaging in unsafe sexual practices. These behaviors are clearly related to cultural prescriptions for men to excel in athletics, ignore safety concerns, drink to excess, fear no illness, and believe that sexual feelings are impulses that are completely out of control. Other, more subtle risky behaviors include: refusing to wear sunscreen, eating unhealthy foods, avoiding exercise or exercising in unhealthy ways, failing to wear seat belts, overworking, not getting enough sleep, and a wide variety of other health-neglecting behaviors.

HOW DO EMOTIONS AFFECT HEALTH?

Recent research has revealed some important connections between emotional styles and physical health. Two particular styles, chronic anger and emotional constriction, are especially problematic, and these two emotional tendencies are much more frequently present in men than in women.[27]

Males are encouraged to keep all feelings completely within their control, except for anger, which, curiously, is seen as out of control. Many people believe that, when a person is angry, he or she needs to "blow off steam"—to express this anger in some way. But a conventional belief can be wrong. In this case, it can be dead wrong. In most circumstances, the unrestrained expression of anger tends to make one more angry, and also tends to damage relationships. In extreme situations, the expression of anger can get a person killed, as in the increasing incidence of "road rage."

Researchers have identified chronic anger as an important contributor to hypertension, heart attack, and recently, stroke. The research on anger expression tells us that "blowing off steam" needs to yield to the wisdom of "counting to ten." As we discussed in Chapter 5, anger is always accompanied by other feelings, usually sadness or fear. "Blowing off steam" never recognizes or resolves the rest of the condition that produced the anger. Failing to do so can only lead men to more anger and continued dissociation, both of which are harmful to health.

Mounting evidence links emotional inexpressiveness to physical health problems and overall adjustment difficulties.[28] *Alexithymia* (literal translation: "no words for feelings") is a condition referring to the inability to know, recognize, or express emotions. As we have stated previously, the dissociative process in men is directly related to decreased awareness of internal affective states, and thus it is related to an increase in alexithymia. This traditionally masculine style of dealing with one's emotional life is detrimental not only to emotional functioning in an intimate relationship but also to the physical well-being of men. Emotions that cannot be recognized or handled appropriately are either stored in the body in stress-related illnesses or unconsciously manifested in unhealthy behaviors. Alexithymia has been linked to alcoholism, low back pain, colitis, arthritis, asthma, and a wide variety of mental health problems.[29]

HOW CAN MEN BETTER
SAFEGUARD THEIR HEALTH?

Given the problems that we have described, some of these answers should be rather obvious. The following suggestions are not intended to be exhaustive, nor are they presented in any particular order. Suffice it to say that men would be well advised to:

- get regular checkups
- learn the symptoms for enlarged prostate, colon cancer, prostate cancer, and other health problems
- conduct regular testicular self-examinations
- use sunscreen
- quit smoking and quit using any tobacco products
- drink alcohol only in moderation
- exercise regularly and healthily (avoid being a "weekend warrior")
- use seat belts
- never drive drunk
- "retire" from dangerous sports such as boxing and football
- control your anger; give appropriate expression to other emotions
- report your symptoms to your physician, and do so honestly
- volunteer important health information even if your doctor does not ask for it
- practice safe sex
- consume less fat and more fruits and vegetables
- take medication when necessary
- learn to relax and use other stress management techniques
- stay home from work when ill
- protect yourself on the job (males account for 94 percent of work-related fatalities)
- store firearms safely or get rid of them
- see a counselor for mental health difficulties
- use your social support system

- drive safely
- maintain an appropriate weight
- stay away from illegal drugs
- pursue healthy recreational pursuits

Given the social demands of masculinity, it is probably impossible for most men to feel completely and absolutely comfortable with all of the behaviors listed above. But one thing that traditional masculinity has taught us is that you don't have to feel completely and absolutely comfortable in order to get something done—we sometimes work or exercise for hours in uncomfortable settings. With regard to health behaviors, the key is not to feel completely comfortable; it is to perform the behavior despite your discomfort, because you are committed to taking care of yourself and being the best you can be in your relationships with others.

It is important to acknowledge that engaging in these behaviors may feel subtly threatening, as they require a man to behave in traditionally unmasculine ways. For example, as we write this chapter, I (C. K.) am only six weeks removed from the shock of my forty-one-year-old brother's fatal heart attack. Besides dealing with my abject grief, I made a commitment to myself and my partner to have a full series of cardiac diagnostic tests, even though I have never had any heart problems, nor do I have any indicators of direct risk such as high cholesterol or hypertension. I do, however, carry the great risk of negative hereditary factors—my father also died of heart disease at a young age.

Despite the fact that I am knowledgeable about men's issues and about men's health, it took me several days to just pick up the phone and make an appointment with my physician. It was easy to let other things get in the way, to conveniently "forget," or to rationalize by saying, "I don't have time" (it took less than three minutes to make the appointment). Looking back, I realize that part of what made me hesitate was the desire to be independent and the fear that physicians might find something to be wrong with my heart. But then I realized that, if something is wrong, I want to know about it, and I want to take steps to prevent health problems. But traditional masculinity encourages me to deny all vulnerability, including physical vulnerability. It also discouraged me from asking for help. I had to make a conscious effort to resist the social pressure to ignore my health.

I (J. L.) have had the opportunity to reexamine my masculine beliefs and behaviors as they affect my family. For instance, I am aware that the school day ends at 3:00 p.m. and the work day ends at or after 5:00 p.m. Before I thought seriously about this difference or participated in a solution to the problems caused by this discrepancy, I assumed that my masculine role was to attend only to my (outside-the-home) work. Blindly following the dictum to "get ahead," I never paused long enough to see that this basic competitive stance (getting ahead *of someone else*) took me away from my family. I saw my place in my family through masculine eyes—family needs defer to work needs, since, after all, that is what pays the bills.

I have come to understand that if I do not reevaluate my masculinity, it will evaluate me, at my family's expense. Writing this book has given me the opportunity to reorganize my work in relation to the larger and more important needs of my family. Unlike many people, I have the luxury of flexible working hours, and I have decided to limit my paid work so that I may be home when my children step off the school bus. I am anxious about this change because I will take a loss in income and because I will be breaking the rules, leaving work halfway through the day, while others continue until 5:00 p.m. or later. At the same time, I am excited about being home in those precious hours after school. Instead of bringing home a tired and spent man to my family, I want my family to come home to a place that nurtures all of us.

The broadest view of relationships with others is in men's connections not only with their friends and families, but also with their co-workers, neighbors, community, culture, and the world at large. Mainstream U. S. culture is highly individualistic. People are encouraged to see all behavior as originating within the individual, but we know that people also have profound effects on one another. We have described how one kind of social pressure influences the compulsive conformity to traditional masculine roles and causes damage to men as well as those who interact with them. As men become gender aware, they can use their considerable social power to work in the opposite direction, toward positive social change.

WHAT IS SOCIAL CHANGE?

Social change describes the slow process of altering beliefs and behaviors in the culture at large. We have seen some evidence of effortful social change within our lifetimes. For example, twenty years ago, many people would never have asked, "Do you mind if I smoke?" Lighting up in a workplace, restaurant, or even a college classroom was so common that most people didn't even give it a second thought, but now people usually assume that smoking is not acceptable under many circumstances. Seat belt use has also changed, and so has making public statements with racist or sexist content. Compared to fifty years ago, many more people are against the use of war as a solution to conflict between countries.

We certainly do not mean to imply that the world has become a fair and safe place. One could easily argue that it is a more hostile world than ever. However, our point is that social attitudes and behaviors can, and sometimes do, change, and that people working together can have positive effects on their communities. Individual men and groups of men can play a special role in contributing to positive social change.

Why Should Individual Men Be Concerned with Social Change?

First, men should be concerned about their wives, friends, and children, all of whom can benefit from positive social change in the area of gender. Second, men have gained tremendous advantages from thousands of years of patriarchy. We believe that this means that we have a responsibility to the world to help others benefit from a sense of empowerment, self-confidence, and appropriate self-assertion. Third, men engaged in pursuits toward bettering other people's lives can feel more engaged and have more of a sense of purpose in the world. If they are depressed, these kinds of feelings will help in the efforts toward healing.

Because of our social, economic, and political power, men are in a unique position to help make the world a better place. For our purposes, we will focus on healing the destructive aspects of traditional masculinity.

WHAT CAN MEN DO TO HELP CHANGE
THE DESTRUCTIVE ASPECTS OF GENDER?

There are several ways in which men can help to turn around some of the damage that has been wrought by narrow gender roles. One of the catch phrases of modern feminism is, "The personal is political." A man's everyday behaviors can help to either maintain or change political and social patterns. People are responsible to one another for the actions that have effects on other people, and men can accept and affirm this responsibility in their daily lives. In Chapter 8, we described one of the most important ways of doing so: by becoming the father that you wanted and deserved in your child-hood. Following are some other suggestions (again, not exhaustive or presented in any specific order):

1. *Confront other men who speak about women in derogatory terms.* Men who make sexist jokes or call women by derogatory names need to know that other men respect women. Negative attitudes toward women are strongly correlated with sexual as-sault, sexual harassment, and domestic violence. These attitudes are reinforced by all male social groups. Men who remain silent when other men display these attitudes passively condone this conduct. Men who speak up, and thereby refuse to be passive bystanders, contribute to attitudinal change in these groups. These kinds of comments are made by men in order to maintain traditional masculinity. As we discussed in Chapter 6, it is in relation to other men that important change can occur.

2. *Support the empowerment of women in the workplace and community.* Gender roles will not become fair until women achieve social, political, and economic power equal to that of men. Men who take gender responsibility seriously strive to communicate respect for women in all of their dealings with them and support their empowerment. It is a myth that women's gains are men's losses. In reality, everyone gains when women are fully empowered.

3. *Refuse to financially support destructive media representations of masculinity.* Action-adventure movies and violent
   television imply that physical aggression is a masculine and
   appropriate way to solve problems. Often, violence is portrayed
   as having no physical, emotional, or financial long-term consequences. In some children's programming (e.g., *Teenage Mu-
   tant Ninja Turtles, Mighty Morphin Power Rangers*), violence
   is also portrayed as *fun!* When you attend to these movies or
   patronize the advertisers of these television shows, you participate in the financial support of these destructive attitudes.
   Support the development of alternative attitudes in the performing arts.

4. *Talk to young men about gender.* Look for "teachable moments" in your interactions with boys and young men. Encourage them to learn about the destructive aspects of masculinity, to
   be who they are, to put sports in an appropriate context in their
   lives, to treat women as equals, and to allow each other the right
   to a full expression of feelings.

5. *Be a role model of healthy masculinity.* Don't limit your life to
   sports and work. Tell others how you feel. Be interested in
   them. Make the choice to be constructive, not destructive.

6. *Participate in community efforts to decrease men's violence
   toward women and children.* Volunteer to help with rape crisis
   or domestic violence organizations. Start a local "White Ribbon Campaign: Men working to end men's violence against
   women" (see the White Ribbon website: www.whiteribbon.ca).

7. *Give financial and other support to organizations that help to
   break down destructive gender stereotypes.*

8. *Talk to male friends about their feelings and about what is
   important in their lives.*

9. *Support political candidates that favor reforms that address
   destructive gender arrangements.*

10. *Use your perceptiveness, creativity, resources, and commit-
    ment to make small changes in the world around you.* Every
    man has a unique set of skills and experiences that he can
    contribute. A little bit of awareness and effort in one's daily
    life can go a long way.

We hope that we have provided a way of thinking about men that you will find useful in your life and/or work. For ourselves, we have become increasingly aware over the years of the impact of gender in our lives. In the process, we have also become aware of choices that we never before knew were available to us. We have been somewhat successful in breaking out of the gender mold in which society and socialization has sought to put us. Although, like everyone, we continue to have struggles, our expansion beyond the limits of traditional masculinity has brought us to lives that are more emotionally compelling, include increasingly richer relationships with our partners and friends, help us to feel more engaged and connected with the world, and allow us to make important contributions to others. As we continue our journey, we wish you well in yours.

Reference Notes

Introduction

1. Real, T. (1997). *I don't want to talk about it: Overcoming the secret legacy of male depression.* New York: Scribner.

2. Osherson, S. (1987). *Finding our fathers: How a man's life is shaped by his relationship with his father.* New York: Ballantine.

3. Herek, G. M. (Ed.). (1996). *Lesbian, gay, and bisexual identities over the life-span: Psychological perspectives.* New York: Oxford University Press; Herek, G. M. (Ed.). (1993). *Psychological perspectives on lesbian and gay male experiences.* New York: Columbia University Press.

4. Blumenfeld, W. J. (Ed.). (1992). *Homophobia: How we all pay the price.* Boston: Beacon.

5. Duberman, M. B. (Ed.). (1997). *Queer representations: Reading lives, reading cultures.* New York University Press.

Chapter 1

1. Sue, D., Sue, D., and Sue, S. (1997). *Understanding abnormal behavior.* Boston: Houghton-Mifflin.

2. American Psychiatric Association (1994). *Diagnostic and statistical manual of mental disorders* (Fourth edition) (DSM-IV). Washington, DC: Author.

3. Strickland, B. R. (1992). Women and depression. *Current Directions in Psychological Science, 1,* 132-135.

4. American Psychiatric Association (1994). *Diagnostic and statistical manual of mental disorders* (Fourth edition) (DSM-IV). Washington, DC: American Psychiatric Association, p. 327.

5. Tavris, C. and Wade, C. (1997). *Psychology in perspective.* New York: Longman.

6. Sue, D., Sue, D., and Sue, S. (1997). *Understanding abnormal behavior.* Boston: Houghton-Mifflin.

7. National Institutes of Mental Health (1985). *Mental Health: United States, 1985.* Washington, DC: U.S. Government Printing Office.

8. Moscicki, E. (1995). Epidemiology of suicidal behavior. *Suicide and Life-Threatening Behavior, 25,* 22-35.

9. Stillion, J. M., McDowell, E. E. and May, J. H. (1989). *Suicide across the life span: Premature exits.* New York: Hemisphere.

10. Sue, D., Sue, D., and Sue, S. (1997). *Understanding abnormal behavior.* Boston: Houghton-Mifflin.

11. Rosenstein, M. and Milazzo-Sayre, L. J. (1981). *Characteristics of admissions to selected mental health facilities, 1975: An annotated book of charts and tables.* Washington, DC: U.S. Government Printing Office.

12. Bloom, B. L. and Caldwell, R. A. (1981). Sex differences in adjustment during the process of marital separation. *Journal of Marriage and the Family, 43,* 693-701; Siegal, J. M. and Kuykendall, D. H. (1990). Loss, widowhood, and psychological distress among the elderly. *Journal of Consulting and Clinical Psychology, 58,* 519-524.

13. United States Bureau of the Census. Statistical abstract of the United States (One-hundred-eleventh edition). Washington, DC: U.S. Government Printing Office.

14. Dolnick, E. (1991, August 13). Why do women outlive men? *The Washington Post Health*, pp. 10-13.

15. Courtenay, W. H. (Under review). Behavioral factors associated with male disease, injury, and death: Evidence and implications for prevention. *Journal of Men's Studies.*

16. Hegelson, V. S. (1990). The role of masculinity in a prognostic predictor of heart attack severity. *Sex Roles, 22,* 755-774.

17. "Anger doubles risk of stroke among men." (1997, November 11). *The Washington Post*, p. A2.

18. Thomas, P. (1994, October 28). U.S. prison population, continuing rapid growth since '80s, surpasses 1 million. *The Washington Post*, p. A3.

19. Browne, A. (1993). Violence against women by male partners: Prevalence, outcomes, and policy implications. *American Psychologist, 48,* 1077-1987.

20. Ibid.

21. Gugliotta, G. (1994, May 16). Institute finds a number that adds up, has meaning on the streets. *The Washington Post*, p. A3.

22. Sue, D., Sue, D., and Sue, S. (1997). *Understanding abnormal behavior.* Boston: Houghton-Mifflin.

Chapter 2

1. Hochschild, A. (1989). *The second shift.* New York: Avon.

2. Pittman, F. (1990). The masculine mystique. *Family Therapy Networker*, May/June, 40-52.

3. Chodorow, N. (1978). *The reproduction of mothering: Psychoanalysis and the sociology of gender.* Berkeley, CA: University of California Press.

4. Lee, J. (1991). *At my father's wedding: Reclaiming our true masculinity.* New York: Bantam.

Chapter 3

1. Bem, S. L. (1993). *The lenses of gender: Transforming the debate on sexual inequality.* New Haven, CT: Yale University Press, pp. 140-141.

2. Rubin, J. Z., Provenzano, F. J., and Luria, Z. (1974). The eye of the beholder: Parents' views on sex of newborns. *American Journal of Orthopsychiatry, 44,* 512-519.

3. Will, J., Self, P., and Datan, N. (1976). Maternal behavior and perceived sex of infant. *American Journal of Orthopsychiatry, 46*, 135-139.

4. Lytton, H. and Romney, D. M. (1991). Parents' differential socialization of boys and girls: A meta-analysis. *Psychological Bulletin, 109*, 267-296.

5. Stoddart, T. and Turiel, E. (1985). Children's concepts of cross-gender activities. *Child Development, 56*, 1241-1252.

6. Kilmartin, C. T. (1994). *The masculine self.* New York: Macmillan.

7. Harlow, H. F. (1958). The nature of love. *American Psychologist, 13*, 673-685.

8. Field, T. (1990). *Infancy.* Cambridge, MA: Harvard University Press.

9. Culp, R. E., Cook, A. S., and Housley, P. C. (1983). A comparison of observed and reported adult-infant interactions: Effects of perceived sex. *Sex Roles, 9*, 475-479.

10. Lytton, H. and Romney, D. M. (1991). Parents' differential socialization of boys and girls: A meta-analysis. *Psychological Bulletin, 109*, 267-296.

11. Block, J. H. (1984). *Sex role identity and ego development.* San Francisco: Jossey-Bass.

12. Basow, S. A. (1992). *Gender: Stereotypes and roles* (Third edition). Pacific Grove, CA: Brooks/Cole.

13. Thorndike, E. L. (1898). Animal intelligence: An experimental study of the associative processes in animals. *Psychological Monographs, 2* (Whole No. 8).

14. Lytton, H. and Romney, D. M. (1991). Parents' differential socialization of boys and girls: A meta-analysis. *Psychological Bulletin, 109*, 267-296.

15. Hartley, R. E. (1959). Sex-role pressures in the socialization of the male child. *Psychological Reports, 5*, 463.

16. Lytton, H. and Romney, D. M. (1991). Parents' differential socialization of boys and girls: A meta-analysis. *Psychological Bulletin, 109*, 267-296.

17. Tavris, C. and Wade, C. (1997). *Psychology in perspective.* New York: Longman.

18. Block, J. H. (1984). *Sex role identity and ego development.* San Francisco: Jossey-Bass.

19. Maccoby, E. E. (1987). Gender as a social construct. Paper presented at the Annual Meeting of the Eastern Psychological Association, Buffalo, NY.

20. Ibid.

21. Emihovich, C. A., Gaier, E. L., and Cronin, N. C. (1984). Sex-role expectations changes by fathers for their sons. *Sex Roles, 11*, 861-868.

22. Basow, S. A. (1992). *Gender: Stereotypes and roles* (Third edition). Pacific Grove, CA: Brooks/Cole.

23. Prothrow-Stith, D. (1993) in interview with *Media and Values, 63*, 6.

24. Polce-Lynch, M., Myers, B. J., Kilmartin, C. T., and Forssmann-Falk, R. (1998). The development of body image, emotional expression, and self-esteem: A qualitative analysis of gender and age patterns. *Sex Roles, 38,* 1025-1048.

25. Brannon, R. (1985). Dimensions of the male sex role in America. In A. G. Sargent (Ed.), *Beyond sex roles* (Second edtion). St. Paul, MN: West, 307.

26. Grief, E. B. (1976). Sex-role playing in preschool children. In J. S. Bruner, A. Jolly, and K. Sylva (Eds.), *Play*. Harmondsworth, England: Penguin.

27. *Discovering Psychology* (1989). "Psychopathology." Program 21 in the video series published by Annenberg/CPB collection. Distributed by Intellimation, Santa Barbara, CA.

28. Skinner, B. F. (1974). *About behaviorism*. New York: Knopf.

29. Basow, S. A. (1992). *Gender: Stereotypes and roles* (Third edition). Pacific Grove, CA: Brooks/Cole.

Chapter 4

1. Coltrane, S. (1998). Theorizing masculinities in contemporary social science. In D. L. Anselmi and A. L. Law (Eds.), *Questions of gender.* Boston: McGraw-Hill, pp. 77-88.

2. Maccoby, E. E. (1990). Gender and relationships: A developmental account. *American Psychologist, 45,* 513-520.

Introduction to Part II

1. Courtenay, W. H. (Under review). Behavioral factors associated with male disease, injury, and death: Evidence and implications for prevention. *Journal of Men's Studies.*

Chapter 6

1. Asch, S. E. (1956). Studies of independence and conformity: A minority of one against a unanimous majority. *Psychological Monographs, 70,* Whole No. 416.

2. Letich, L. (1991, May/June). Do you know who your friends are? *Utne Reader,* 85-87.

Chapter 7

1. Bem, S. L. (1993). *The lenses of gender: Transforming the debate on sexual inequality.* New Haven, CT: Yale University Press.

Chapter 9

1. Hoffman, J. (1992, February 16). When men hit women. *The New York Times Magazine,* pp. 23-27, 64-66, 72.

2. Colburn, D. (1994, June 28). Domestic violence: AMA president decries a major public health problem. *The Washington Post Health,* pp. 10-12.

3. Ibid.

4. FBI (1994). *Uniform crime reports.* Washington, DC: U.S. Government Printing Office.

5. Parrot, A. and Bechofer, L. (1991). *Acquaintance rape: The hidden crime.* New York: Wiley.

6. Hoffman, J. (1992, February 16). When men hit women. *The New York Times Magazine,* pp. 23-27, 64-66, 72.

7. Biden, J. R. (1993). Violence against women: The congressional response. *American Psychologist, 48,* 1059-1061.

8. Lisak, D. (1993). Sexual assault: Perpetrator characteristics and solutions. Paper presented at Mary Washington College, November 18.

9. Lisak, D. (1991). Sexual aggression, masculinity, and fathers. *Signs, 16,* 238-262.

10. Lisak, D. (1993). Sexual assault: Perpetrator characteristics and solutions. Paper presented at Mary Washington College, November 18.

11. FBI (1994). *Uniform crime reports.* Washington, DC: U.S. Government Printing Office.

12. Gondolf, E. W. (1988). Who are those guys? Toward a behavioral typology of batterers. *Violence and Victims, 3,* 187-203.

13. Browne, A. (1993). Violence against women by male partners: Prevalence, outcomes, and policy implications. *American Psychologist, 48,* 1077-1987.

14. Landes, A. B., Squyres, S., and Quiram, J. (Eds.). (1997). *Violent relationships: Battering and abuse among adults.* Wylie, TX: Information Plus.

15. Gondolf, E. W. (1988). Who are those guys? Toward a behavioral typology of batterers. *Violence and Victims, 3,* 187-203.

Chapter 10

1. Kilmartin, C. T. (1994). *The masculine self.* New York: Macmillan.

2. United States Bureau of the Census (1995). *Statistical abstract of the United States* (One-hundred-fifteenth edition). Washington, DC: U.S. Government Printing Office.

3. Dolnick, E. (1991, August 13). Why do women outlive men? *The Washington Post Health,* pp. 10-13.

4. Harrison, J., Chin, J., and Ficarotto, T. (1995). Warning: Masculinity may be dangerous to your health. In M. S. Kimmel and M. A. Messner (Eds.), *Men's lives* (Third edition, pp. 237-249). Boston: Allyn and Bacon.

5. Ibid.

6. Ibid.

7. Moscicki, E. (1995). Epidemiology of suicidal behavior. *Suicide and Life-Threatening Behavior, 25,* 22-35.

8. Harrison, J., Chin, J., and Ficarotto, T. (1995). Warning: Masculinity may be dangerous to your health. In M. S. Kimmel and M. A. Messner (Eds.), *Men's lives* (Third edition, pp. 237-249). Boston: Allyn and Bacon.

9. Courtenay, W. H. (Under review). Behavioral factors associated with male disease, injury, and death: Evidence and implications for prevention. *Journal of Men's Studies.*

10. Dolnick, E. (1991, August 13). Why do women outlive men? *The Washington Post Health*, pp. 10-13.

11. Ibid.

12. Harrison, J., Chin, J., and Ficarotto, T. (1995). Warning: Masculinity may be dangerous to your health. In M. S. Kimmel and M. A. Messner (Eds.), *Men's lives* (Third edition, pp. 237-249). Boston: Allyn and Bacon.

13. Courtenay, W. H. (Under review). Behavioral factors associated with male disease, injury, and death: Evidence and implications for prevention. *Journal of Men's Studies.*

14. Harrison, J., Chin, J., and Ficarotto. T. (1995). Warning: Masculinity may be dangerous to your health. In M. S. Kimmel and M. A. Messner (Eds.), *Men's lives* (Third edition, pp. 237-249). Boston: Allyn and Bacon.

15. Colburn, D. (1993, October 19). Chewing tobacco: A baseball tradition that can be deadly. *The Washington Post Health,* pp. 13-15.

16. Sue, D., Sue, D., and Sue, S. (1997). *Understanding abnormal behavior.* Boston: Houghton-Mifflin.

17. Ibid.

18. Moscicki, E. (1995). Epidemiology of suicidal behavior. *Suicide and Life-Threatening Behavior, 25,* 22-35.

19. Garland, A. F., and Zigler, E. (1993). Adolescent suicide prevention: Current research and social policy implications. *American Psychologist, 48,* 169-182.

20. Ibid.

21. National Center for Health Statistics (1989). *Vital statistics of the United States 1987 (Volume 2): Mortality.* Washington, DC: U.S. Government Printing Office.

22. Hackett, T. P., Rosenbaum, J. F., and Cassen, N. H. (1985). Cardiovascular disorders. In H. I. Kaplan and B. J. Saddock (Eds.). *Comprehensive textbook of psychiatry* (Fourth edition, pp. 1148-1159). Baltimore: Williams and Wilkins.

23. Herman, R. (1992). The cancer men didn't talk about . . . until now. *The Washington Post Health,* pp. 10-13.

24. Adler, J., Rosenberg, D., and Springen, K. (1993, December 27). The killer we don't discuss. *Newsweek, 122,* pp. 40-41.

25. Brott, A. (1994, June 10). Tough guys die sooner. *Washington Post,* p. D5.

26. Ibid.

27. Kilmartin, C. T. (1994). *The masculine self.* New York: Macmillan; Eisler, R. M., Skidmore, J. R., and Ward, C. H. (1988). Masculine gender role stress: Predictor of anger, anxiety, and health-risk behaviors. *Journal of Personality Assessment, 52,* 133-141.

28. Kilmartin, C. T. (1994). *The masculine self.* New York: Macmillan.

29. Ibid.; Kinder, B. N., and Curtiss, G. (1990). Alexithymia among empirically derived subgroups of chronic back pain patients. *Journal of Personality Assessment, 54,* 351-362.

Index

Order Your Own Copy of
This Important Book for Your Personal Library!

THE PAIN BEHIND THE MASK
Overcoming Masculine Depression

_____ in hardbound at $39.95 (ISBN: 0-7890-0557-3)

_____ in softbound at $19.95 (ISBN: 0-7890-0558-1)

COST OF BOOKS_____

OUTSIDE USA/CANADA/
MEXICO: ADD 20%_____

POSTAGE & HANDLING_____
(US: $3.00 for first book & $1.25
for each additional book)
Outside US: $4.75 for first book
& $1.75 for each additional book)

SUBTOTAL_____

IN CANADA: ADD 7% GST_____

STATE TAX_____
(NY, OH & MN residents, please
add appropriate local sales tax)

FINAL TOTAL_____
(If paying in Canadian funds,
convert using the current
exchange rate. UNESCO
coupons welcome.)

☐ **BILL ME LATER:** ($5 service charge will be added)
(Bill-me option is good on US/Canada/Mexico orders only;
not good to jobbers, wholesalers, or subscription agencies.)

☐ Check here if billing address is different from
shipping address and attach purchase order and
billing address information.

Signature _____

☐ **PAYMENT ENCLOSED: $**_____

☐ **PLEASE CHARGE TO MY CREDIT CARD.**

☐ Visa ☐ MasterCard ☐ AmEx ☐ Discover

Account # _____

Exp. Date _____

Signature _____

Prices in US dollars and subject to change without notice.

NAME _____

INSTITUTION _____

ADDRESS _____

CITY _____

STATE/ZIP _____

COUNTRY _____ COUNTY (NY residents only) _____

TEL _____ FAX _____

E-MAIL_____
May we use your e-mail address for confirmations and other types of information? ☐ Yes   ☐ No

Order From Your Local Bookstore or Directly From
The Haworth Press, Inc.
10 Alice Street, Binghamton, New York 13904-1580 • USA
TELEPHONE: 1-800-HAWORTH (1-800-429-6784) / Outside US/Canada: (607) 722-5857
FAX: 1-800-895-0582 / Outside US/Canada: (607) 772-6362
E-mail: getinfo@haworthpressinc.com
PLEASE PHOTOCOPY THIS FORM FOR YOUR PERSONAL USE.

BOF96